It Happened In the Civil War

Remarkable Events That Shaped History

Second Edition

Michael R. Bradley

gpp

Guilford, Connecticut

Project editor: Gregory Hyman
Layout: Joanna Beyer

The Library of Congress has cataloged the previous edition as follows:

Bradley, Michael R. (Michael Raymond), 1940-
  It happened in the Civil War/Michael R. Bradley.
    p. cm.—(It happened in series)
  Includes bibliographical references and index.
  ISBN-13: 978-0-7627-1165-9
    1. United States—History—Civil War, 1861-1865—Anecdotes. 2. United
  States—History—Civil War, 1861-1865—Social aspects—Anecdotes.
  3. United States—History—Civil War, 1861-1865—Biography—Anecdotes.
  I. Title. II. Series
  E655.B7 2002
  973.7—dc21   2001040578

ISBN 978-0-7627-5872-2

Printed in the United States of America

10 9 8 7 6 5 4 3 2 1

CONTENTS

CONTENTS

PREFACE

You hold in your hands a most unusual book. *It Happened in the Civil War* is unlike most any other book you have seen concerning the Civil War, a conflict that has been called "the American *Iliad.*" This book is not a trivia collection, an assembling of odd facts and figures about the war; it deals with things more important than that. Neither is it a general history of the sectional conflict, for while battles and campaigns may be mentioned, they are not the focus of this work. Also this volume avoids the historians' argument, "What caused the war?" That argument has been going on since 1861 and shows no signs of being resolved. Advocating a position on a particular historical controversy is not the purpose of this book either. The war has produced countless historical controversies, and few—if any—of them have been brought to a conclusion.

So what is this book? This is a collection of true stories that go behind the scenes of history to highlight some lesser-known and unusual happenings that shaped the course of the war and the lives of men and women in the North and the South. Here you'll find the stories of real decisions by real people who faced both a national and personal crisis and rose to the occasion. These stories take you into the war and introduce you to some of the people whose lives were touched by it.

Be prepared for some surprises when you read this book. The realities of those days were not so simple as we today assume. The passage of time has obscured the reality of the past with stereotypes.

PREFACE

In these pages you'll discover things you didn't know about the war, and the things you think you know will be challenged.

Read this book to learn about yourself, for we today are not so very different from the people you will meet in these pages. Whether you are from the North or the South or from another country; whether you are of African, European, or Native American ancestry; whether you are male or female, you will find something of yourself in these stories. And you will be surprised by some of the things that truly happened in the American Civil War.

THE DOUBLE LIFE OF
EMMA SEELYE

1861–62

Among the units that poured into Washington, D.C., in June 1861 was the Second Michigan Infantry. Company F of that regiment carried on its rolls a slightly built young man named Franklin Thompson, usually called Frank. Because he seemed to have special talents for the work, Frank was assigned to hospital duty and to carry the regimental mail. Frank would later say that he felt he had learned nursing skills from his mother. It was also often commented that he had a special ability to calm nervous, agitated men, almost as if a current flowed through his hands.

Both hospital work and mail carrying involved an element of danger. At the battle of First Manassas, the Union hospitals were overrun by the Confederates, and Frank found himself behind enemy lines. It was only with difficulty and daring that he made his way back to friendly territory.

Perhaps it was the initiative shown on this occasion that caused the colonel commanding the Second Michigan, Orlando Poe, to name Frank mail carrier. The duties associated with this position required Frank Thompson to be out of camp frequently, and the position was an excellent "cover" for actually being a scout sent to penetrate Confederate lines.

In the spring of 1862, as McClellan's army advanced up the Virginia Peninsula toward Richmond, Frank was sent to penetrate the Confederate lines near Yorktown. Disguising himself as a slave, Frank not only entered the Confederate lines, he was conscripted to help build fortifications. Because of his small stature, he was assigned the task of carrying water to work parties. A couple days of this chore gave him a thorough knowledge of the design of the fortifications, and Frank tried to slip back to Union lines with this information. Along the way he was apprehended by a Confederate officer who gave him a rifle and ordered him to take his place in advance of the lines as a picket guard, a duty often assigned to slaves.

Slipping away from his guard post after dark, Frank took his news to Union headquarters, only to be asked to go back into the Confederate lines again. This time Frank assumed the guise of an Irish woman and peddled cakes and pies throughout the Southern ranks. In his travels Frank found himself spending the night in an otherwise deserted house with a dying Confederate officer. With his dying words this officer asked Frank to deliver his watch to a friend on the staff of Confederate General Richard Ewell. Frank gladly accepted this chance to enter a Confederate headquarters, and soon he was back in Union lines with even more valuable information.

In recognition of his reconnaissance services, Frank was officially relieved from infantry duty and made a courier on the staff of General Philip Kearny. In this capacity he was injured when his horse, maddened by the noise of battle, bit him severely on the shoulder and kicked him with both hind feet at once.

Following the Seven Days' Battles and the Union retreat from the Peninsula, Frank was asked by General Samuel P. Heintzelman to penetrate Confederate lines again. This time Frank went disguised as a black woman who was going south to look for friends. Soon he had been hired as a cook at a Confederate camp. Three times in ten days Frank crossed the lines with news of Southern plans. Despite his information the Union army, now under the command of General John Pope, found itself badly outmaneuvered and outgeneraled by the Confederate commanders, Robert E. Lee and "Stonewall" Jackson. When Jackson destroyed Pope's base of supplies at Manassas Junction, a second bloody battle was fought over the same hills and fields where Frank and the Second Michigan had been in July of 1861. During the Union retreat toward Washington, General Kearny was killed while Frank was riding by his side. No longer a courier, Frank returned to his regiment and again worked in the hospitals as his unit camped near the capital.

The Second Michigan did not fight at Sharpsburg but remained on garrison duty in Washington, during which time Frank volunteered to go to the battlefield to help nurse the wounded. The veteran regiment was sent into the fiercest part of the battle at Fredericksburg, Virginia, in December 1862, and again Frank left his place on the firing line when the guns fell silent to report to the hospital, where thousands of men lay bleeding and dying. In January 1863 the Second Michigan was part of the army corps of General Ambrose Burnside that was sent to Kentucky. There Frank continued to engage in scouting activities and in secret operations against the numerous Confederate sympathizers who gave support to roving bands of Southern cavalry, which were swarming all over the state. On one occasion while working undercover, Frank was swept up by one of these units and was on the verge of being sworn into the Confederate army when he managed to escape. In April 1863 Frank was sent to the hospital with a severe case of malaria. He asked for a furlough so that he could recuperate at home but was refused leave. That same night he deserted his regiment, never to be seen again—at least not as Frank Thompson.

In 1864 *Nurse and Spy* was published in Hartford, Connecticut. This book told the rest of the story of Frank Thompson. Frank was really Sarah Emma Edmonds. She had deserted because she knew that in the hospital her gender would be discovered. But being devoted to the Union cause, Emma went to Harpers Ferry, Virginia, once she had recovered from malaria and went to work for the Christian Commission in the hospitals there. She continued this work until the end of the war.

While in Harpers Ferry, Emma met Linus Seelye, a carpenter from New Brunswick, Canada. The two were married in 1867 and were soon working for the Freedmen's Bureau. In the employ of this government agency, they moved around a lot but lived for several years in Louisiana, where they helped run an orphans' home and school. Later, while living in Fort Scott, Kansas, Emma produced documents and told details that proved she was Frank Thompson. She even visited old comrades, many of whom could still recognize her voice, but few of whom were at first able to convince themselves that this middle-aged matron was the same young soldier with whom they had marched and fought in the war.

On July 5, 1884, the Congress of the United States sent to the president a bill that would remove the charge of desertion from the record of Frank Thompson and would give Emma Seelye a soldier's pension. In 1897 Emma became the only woman ever to be granted membership in the Union army's veterans' organization, the Grand Army of the Republic (GAR).

On September 5, 1898, Emma died in a town near Houston, Texas. Her funeral was conducted by the local GAR camp, who buried her in their cemetery in Houston. Today Emma lies under a tombstone with the simple inscription:

EMMA SEELYE

ARMY NURSE

A CHINESE CONFEDERATE
AT FORT DONELSON

1862

Charles Marshall was not at all happy about his surroundings. Just seconds before, he had heard a loud "bang" down the river from where he sat in his tent. The "bang" was followed by a moaning shriek that got louder and louder until it ended in a thunderous "boom" right over his head and shards of iron came whistling out of the smoke of the explosion. Charles Marshall quickly exchanged his tent for a wet, muddy hole in the ground as more and more shells from the Yankee gunboats exploded over Fort Donelson.

Although everyone knew him as "Charles Marshall" from Huntsville, Alabama, his name actually was Dzau Tse-Zeh and he had been born near Shanghai about 1845. So, what was this Chinese youth doing in a Confederate unit at Fort Donelson in Tennessee?

Tse-Zeh was the son of a poor man with a large family. When his father died, about 1850, Tse-Zeh went to live with an older brother who worked in Shanghai. A friend of the older brother introduced the boy to the Reverend James W. Lambuth, a missionary of the

Methodist Church. Tse-Zeh liked Rev. Lambuth and, in time, came to accept the religious beliefs of the Methodist Episcopal Church, South. Shortly after his introduction to Rev. Lambuth, another missionary couple arrived, Dr. and Mrs. David C. Kelley.

Tse-Zeh became a valuable part of the church activities led by the Lambuth and Kelley families. He helped with the chores around their households, assisted with the services they conducted in their church, and helped teach the Kelleys Chinese. Dr. and Mrs. Kelley had lost a child, their firstborn, while on the voyage to China and, in some ways, Tse-Zeh became the child they did not have.

In 1859 the Lambuth and Kelley families were ready to return to the United States on furlough. Tse-Zeh was an intelligent young lad, possessed of a desire to continue his education so he could improve life in China, and he had a strong sense of adventure. Not long before the missionaries departed, Tse-Zeh asked to go to the United States with them, and they agreed.

The trip from Shanghai to New Orleans was long and tedious, but once their ship docked in the Crescent City, there was a lot to see. The party boarded a riverboat for the trip to Vicksburg, near the home of the Lambuths. In Vicksburg, Tse-Zeh met the well-known Methodist pastor Rev. Charles Marshall. Tse-Zeh decided he would take that name for the duration of his stay in the States. From Vicksburg, the Kelleys and Charles Marshall traveled by riverboat up the Mississippi to the mouth of the Ohio, then up the Ohio to the Tennessee, and finally, up the Tennessee to Whitesburg Landing, just a few miles south of Huntsville, Alabama. There, Rev. Kelley was to take up his duties as the pastor of the First Methodist Church.

Tse-Zeh, or Charles Marshall, studied hard in Huntsville, reading theological works and studying medicine by assisting some of the local doctors.

On January 11, 1861, Alabama seceded from the Union and preparations for war began. Dr. Kelley raised a company of cavalry from among the men of his congregation and they took the name Kelley Troopers. After a summer of training and drill, the men were ready to go to war. Just before leaving Huntsville for Memphis, Dr. Kelley asked Tse-Zeh if he would like to accompany the men as a personal aide to Kelley. As an aide, Tse-Zeh would assist with camp chores and take a role in religious services whenever Kelley had a chance to conduct them. Tse-Zeh's sense of adventure led him to agree to go, and Charles Marshall became a member of the Kelley Troopers.

In Memphis, Captain Kelley, as the reverend now was, and his men joined the cavalry regiment being organized by Nathan Bedford Forrest. This is how Charles Marshall came to be at Fort Donelson.

Marshall had seen duty in the field prior to Fort Donelson as he accompanied Forrest's regiment of cavalry on marches and in skirmishes in western Kentucky in November and December 1861. This service included a sharp engagement at the town of Sacramento, Kentucky, where Marshall and Kelley led an attack on the flank of the Union line, breaking the line and then pursuing the retreating Yankees. Marshall became well acquainted with Forrest himself when Kelley was promoted to major and named the adjutant of the regiment. In this capacity, Kelley shared with Forrest a tent as their sleeping quarters and Marshall attended both the men; he also ate at the table with Kelley and Forrest. None of this limited military experience prepared Marshall for being in a fort under bombardment by eight heavily armed U.S. gunboats.

For all their noise and smoke, the gunboats didn't do the fort a great deal of damage, and at the end of the days' fighting, the battered ironclads retreated down the Cumberland River. The horror of the bombardment was nothing compared to that experienced by Marshall on the following day as the Confederates attacked the surrounding U.S. forces. All day Forrest and Kelley were in the thick of the battle, and Marshall was never far from Kelley's side. By the end of the day, the dead and wounded lay thick on the freezing ground and puddles of blood were congealing in the snow. Marshall had seen and heard things beyond his imagination. Among the thousands of men in the two armies gathered about the fort there were two who could discuss the events of the day in Chinese—Charles Marshall and David Kelley.

Despite their initial success, the Confederates found themselves trapped in the fort and it was decided they should surrender—all of them except the command of Bedford Forrest. On the night before the surrender, Forrest led his command, including Charles Marshall, through the freezing water of a lonely ford on a backwater of the Cumberland River to escape to Nashville. Following the suffering and death of battle, now came the danger and discomfort of a march in wet clothes in bitterly cold weather.

This was enough of war for Charles Marshall. In early March the command of Bedford Forrest was in Huntsville, Alabama. Marshall requested to be discharged and sent to live with the Lambuths at Jackson, Mississippi. This request was granted.

In 1864 the Lambuth family, accompanied by Marshall, received a pass through the lines to travel to New York City on the first leg of a return journey to China. They traveled by boat from Vicksburg to Nashville, then by rail to Louisville and on to New York. As their riverboat passed the site of Fort Donelson on its way to Nashville, Charles Marshall recounted to the Lambuth family the story of his service in the battle there.

That story was recounted many times to other audiences, for Marshall returned to his native land and became the superintendent of the Soochow Hospital, where he told generations of medical students about his experience as a Confederate soldier. Following the war, David Kelley became secretary of the Board of Missions of the Methodist Church in the South and had the opportunity to keep in touch with his former aide, Tse-Zeh, a Chinese Confederate.

THE DEATH OF THE WOODEN NAVY

1862

It was just before 12:45 p.m. on March 8, 1862, when the wooden navy died. At that hour the quartermaster of the USS *Congress* saw a strange sight coming out of the Elizabeth River into Hampton Roads. Turning to a nearby officer he said, "Sir, I wish you would take a look over there. I believe that thing is a-coming out." "That thing" was the CSS *Virginia*, the first oceangoing armored vessel to go into combat on tidal water. Two hundred sixty-two feet bow to stern, with a 178-square-foot casemate shaped like the gabled roof of a house, this ship was built out of four-inch-thick iron plates bolted onto a solid timber frame two feet thick. The muzzles of two 6.4-inch rifled cannon and four smoothbore cannon that fired eight-inch shells and balls projected from four gun ports on each side. At the bow and stern ends of the casemate, a seven-inch rifled cannon was mounted on a pivot so it could be turned to fire through any one of three gun ports. The *Virginia* glistened in the noonday sun as she slowly steamed across Hampton Roads because her iron sides, sloping at a thirty-six-degree angle, had been liberally smeared with grease in the hope this would cause enemy cannon shot to skid off her sides. Her 320-man crew waited in silence for the range to close.

Actually, the CSS *Virginia* was the resurrected USS *Merrimack,* a ship that had been in the Norfolk naval yard for repairs when Virginia seceded. To prevent the ship from falling into Confederate hands, U.S. authorities set fire to her before abandoning the yard. Although the ship was burned to the waterline, the Confederates had raised the hull, cut away the burned portions, and built an iron shell atop the hull.

Some two hundred yards north of where the Congress was sitting, the USS *Cumberland* swung to anchor. Lieutenant Thomas O. Selfridge spotted the approaching *Virginia* about the same time his friends aboard the *Congress* did. Quickly, the drummers on both vessels began to sound "Beat to Quarters," and sailors rushed to prepare the ships for action. The most obvious problem they faced was that both the *Congress* and the *Cumberland* were wooden sailing ships. During the coming engagement both would be almost stationary.

The commander of the *Cumberland,* Lieutenant George Morris, ordered one of his tenders, the *Zouave,* to steam out to meet and fire on the *Virginia.* Acting Master Henry Reaney went forward boldly, although his ship was armed with only a single cannon. As soon as he reached the proper distance, Reaney opened fire, sending six shots flying across the waves toward the *Virginia.* The iron behemoth steamed calmly along, ignoring *Zouave* as the thirty-pound iron balls bounced harmlessly off her sides.

By 2:00 p.m. the *Virginia* was nearing the *Cumberland* and *Congress. Virginia's* commanding officer, Captain Franklin Buchanan, had already told his officers he intended to ram the *Cumberland* with the huge iron beak bolted on the bow. Ironically, in this first engagement where a modern armored ship gave battle, the tactics used would have been familiar to Greek sailors from 2,500 years earlier.

As the *Virginia* slowly bore down on the *Cumberland,* every gun on the Union vessels opened fire. By now the *Saint Lawrence* was coming up to help, and the three U.S. ships were bringing to the fight 124 cannon, 22 of them capable of firing balls nine inches in diameter, and over one thousand men. But the *Virginia* had one insuperable advantage: Surrounding her ten cannon and 320 men were four inches of iron.

Ignoring the storm of gunfire, the *Virginia* steamed ahead until only yards separated her from the *Cumberland.* Then, with a crunch, the iron beak cleaved into the side of the U.S. vessel. Immediately, the *Cumberland* started down—taking the *Virginia* with her! The iron beak was stuck fast in the hull of the *Cumberland.* Finally, as the downward angle increased, there came a wrenching sound and the prow broke free.

Then the *Congress* became the target. Aboard her Lieutenant Joseph Smith ordered sails set and signaled the *Zouave* to come help tow his ship. The wind was too light for the *Congress* to escape, but Lieutenant Smith hoped to get to water too shallow for the *Virginia* to navigate. This was a helpful move, but the *Congress* could not escape the hail of iron flying about her. As she made for the shore, the *Congress* was riddled with cannon balls, Lieutenant Smith was killed, and the ship set on fire in several places. When the news of the battle reached the North, Lieutenant Smith's father said, "The *Congress* surrendered? Then Joe is dead."

All over Hampton Roads other U.S. warships tried to move to the aid of those under attack, but light winds hampered the wooden sailing ships, and shallow water caused several of the steamers to run aground. With no help available, the *Congress* struck her flag in surrender. However, as the sailors from the *Virginia* tried to board the burning ship, Union troops onshore continued to fire, so neither side occupied the *Congress.* She would burn for several hours before blowing up about midnight.

Now the crew of the *Virginia* had a difficult decision to make. Her captain, Franklin Buchanan, had been wounded in the thigh by a rifle ball during the attack on the *Congress.* The day was coming to an end, and the tide was falling. Should the *Virginia* continue to fight after dark, risking running aground, or was it better to withdraw for the night and finish the job the next day? Not far away lay the biggest prize of all, the USS *Minnesota,* a frigate carrying fifty-eight guns, and she was stuck fast in the mud. There were no U.S. ships left nearby to come help her.

Despite the *Minnesota's* defenseless position, the *Virginia* withdrew. But the next day would not see her finish the job. Just as the *Virginia* was withdrawing, a curious little vessel named the USS *Monitor* was entering Hampton Roads. Designed by John Ericsson, and sometimes described as "a tin can on a shingle," the ironclad *Monitor* mounted only two eleven-inch cannon, but they were contained in a revolving turret. This meant the guns could be trained on a new target without turning the entire ship. Also, the *Monitor* was fast and maneuverable, while the *Virginia* was slow and cumbersome. The next day the *Virginia* and the *Monitor* would batter each other for four hours, sometimes while touching each other, without either doing serious damage to the other. From that day forward ships would be made of iron. On March 8, 1862, the age of "wooden ships, iron men" came to an end.

EXPERIENCES AT SHILOH
INSPIRE A GREAT NOVEL

1862

Major General Lew Wallace knew he needed to get his Third Division to Pittsburg Landing, Tennessee. Specifically, he knew he was needed a few miles south of the Landing near a little Methodist church named Shiloh Chapel. "Curious name for a place where a battle is raging," thought Wallace, "Shiloh means 'place of peace.'" But as his ears told him, there was no peace at Shiloh that morning of April 6, 1862.

The outbreak of a battle did not surprise Wallace. In this he was alone in the Union high command. Commanding general Ulysses S. Grant was not expecting a battle. He had scattered his army over several square miles around Pittsburg Landing without ordering them to fortify their positions and without posting a good cavalry screen between his camps and Corinth, Mississippi, where the Confederate army was concentrated. Grant even kept his headquarters in Savannah, Tennessee, several miles from the camps of his men. William Tecumseh Sherman had not been vigilant on his sector of the line around Shiloh Church. His camps had been hit by a surprise attack early on the morning of the 6th, his men caught just as they were rolling out of their blankets. But Wallace was expecting a battle and was ready for one. He hoped Grant and Sherman would recover from their surprise; after all, they were his friends as well as his fellow officers.

Wallace had led his division of Grant's army to the village of Crump's Landing on March 13. He was under orders to advance westward to wreck the Mobile and Ohio Railroad, a task he had accomplished easily. Almost every day since then, however, his men had skirmished with Confederate infantry commanded by General Benjamin Franklin Cheatham. Wallace knew the Confederates were nearby and that they were aggressive. In order to be better prepared to meet a Confederate attack from either the southwest or west, Wallace left a small force of his men at Crump's Landing on the Tennessee River and moved the rest a couple of miles west to a small hamlet called Stony Lonesome. He then sent out work parties to improve a local road that led from Stony Lonesome to Shiloh Church, the front-line position of his friend William Sherman.

This move gave Wallace access to two roads leading to the main army. He could march from Stony Lonesome back to Crump's Landing and then south along the winding, muddy, low-lying River Road to Pittsburg Landing, or he could follow the improved local road from Stony Lonesome to Shiloh Church. The force Wallace had left at Crump's Landing gave him easy communication with Grant's headquarters in Savannah, Tennessee. Lew Wallace was prepared for battle.

In the midst of all this work, there had been some intellectually stimulating moments. The commander of the Eleventh Illinois Cavalry was Colonel Robert Ingersoll, a man with a national reputation as an agnostic who had traveled widely lecturing on his belief that the existence of God could not be proved. The views of Colonel Ingersoll had prompted Wallace to engage in a study of religion, a topic he found fascinating. Wallace became intensely interested in the life of Jesus Christ.

On April 6 the battle began at first light as the Confederate army, having advanced undetected from Corinth, hit the unsuspecting and unprepared Union lines. By 6:00 a.m. Lew Wallace was awakened by the noise of the distant fight. Dressing and mounting his horse, he rode to Crump's Landing to await orders. About 9:00 a.m. Grant's command boat, the *Tigress,* paused at the Landing and Wallace was instructed to be ready to march as soon as orders arrived. Grant then went on to Pittsburg Landing.

Reaching the main body of his army, Grant found a desperate situation. He immediately sent a courier to Crump's Landing with orders for Wallace to move to Sherman's aid on the right flank of the Union army. The order reached Wallace at 11:30 a.m. and he moved out quickly.

On the battlefield, the situation for the Union forces deteriorated quickly. The Confederates piled more and more men into their attack and the Union forces steadily fell back. Sherman had to abandon his position around Shiloh Church and retreat some 800 yards. As Wallace reached the edge of the fighting, a messenger dashed up with discouraging news. The U.S. forces under Sherman no longer controlled the terminus of the road over which he was marching. If he continued as he was going, Wallace's division would slam into the Confederate army. His attack might divert the Confederates or it might result in Wallace's troops being surrounded and wiped out. The best choice was for Wallace to turn around his division, march back to Stony Lonesome, and then proceed to Crump's Landing to take the River Road. All afternoon frantic messengers from Grant reached Wallace, telling him to hurry. But Wallace was traveling over crowded, muddy, partially flooded roads. "Hurry" could not be done rapidly! It was 6:30 p.m., after dark, when Wallace arrived. None of this was his fault; indeed, he had been better prepared for battle than most any other U.S. general.

During the night, Wallace put his men in position on the Union right flank. At daybreak, April 7, his men led the counterattack that retook the battlefield and forced the Confederates into retreat. Shiloh was a Union victory in the sense that the Confederate attack had been repulsed, but the fact that the attack had caught Grant, Sherman, and others unaware raised embarrassing questions. In an attempt to deflect these questions, Wallace became the scapegoat. If he had been better prepared, if he had marched faster, if he had used a different road, it was said, the army would not have been forced back nor would it have lost so many men. Although he had made his preparations properly, somehow it was all the fault of Wallace.

Grant and Sherman did not come to the defense of Wallace; instead, they were among those placing blame on him. As a result of this criticism, Wallace was sent to the rear and held only minor commands for the rest of the war. "As a rule," he would write, "there is no surer way to the dislike of men than to behave well when they have behaved badly." The only other significant action in which Wallace participated was at the Battle of Monocacy River in the summer of 1864, when a Confederate force under General Jubal A. Early made a raid into Maryland that briefly brought Southern troops in sight of the capitol building. After the war, he was a member of the court-martial that tried those accused in the plot to assassinate President Lincoln and he was on the court that condemned Major Henry Wirz, the commander of the Confederate prison camp at Andersonville.

Wallace never forgot his Shiloh experience and his unfair treatment. Neither did he forget his religious studies. In 1880 Lew Wallace published *Ben-Hur: A Tale of the Christ,* a book in which the hero is betrayed by false friends. At last the hero gets his revenge while also becoming a follower of Jesus.

Ben-Hur became the best-selling American novel of the nineteenth century and was not surpassed in sales until the publication of *Gone With the Wind.* The book has never been out of print since its first publication and has been made into a movie four times.

AN UNUSUAL AIR FORCE

1862

He was on in years now, Lee's "Old War Horse," Lieutenant General James Longstreet. Perhaps his memory had grown a bit dim, or maybe he just wanted to tell a good tale. At any rate, he took up his pen and wrote for the editors of *Battles and Leaders,*

> *The Federals had been using balloons in examining our positions, and we watched with envious eyes these beautiful observatories. . . . A genius suggested we send out and gather all the silk dresses in the Confederacy and make a balloon. Soon we had a ship of many and varied hues. . . . One day our balloon was on a steamer going down the James River when the tide went out and left our vessel and balloon high and dry on a bar. The Federals gathered it in, and with it, the last silk dress in the Confederacy. This was the meanest trick of the war.*

Like so many tales about the Civil War, this one contains a lot of romance and a kernel of truth. The truth is that the Civil War did indeed produce an "air force" (or, at least, a balloon force), and that both the Union and the Confederacy had one. But the Confederacy was not so starved for resources that Southern women had to give up their silk dresses to manufacture a balloon. The truth, however, does provide a fascinating story.

Early in the war, Thaddeus Lowe offered his scientific services to the United States, his purpose being to use hydrogen-filled balloons to ascend high over camps and battlefields to spy on the enemy. Lowe even developed a series of copper-lined wooden tanks that could be mounted on wagons. In these tanks he combined the ingredients that produced hydrogen so his balloons could be filled with gas on the battlefield.

Unfortunately, there were difficulties in sending messages from the balloon to the ground. Often the "signaling device" was something as crude as tying a note to a rock and throwing it over the side of the basket in which the observer hung beneath the balloon. Because no one in the United States Army had ever used a balloon, there were no trained observers who could interpret what they were seeing. Troop movements were hard to predict. Maneuvers were obscured by the dust and smoke of battle or hidden by the wooded terrain. Yet when the Union tried a new device, the Confederates felt obligated to match it as nearly as they could. So when Thaddeus Lowe's balloons appeared over the flat countryside of the Virginia Peninsula in the spring of 1862, the Southerners went to work.

The first problem for the rebels was obtaining gas. Hydrogen gas is generated by using a large amount of sulfuric acid, which comes from sulfur. The South had sulfur, but that chemical was a major ingredient in manufacturing gunpowder. The Confederate high command did not think it wise to divert sulfur from gunpowder to use in balloons. Fortunately for those who were working to form the primitive air force, there were other ways of raising a balloon. Hot air was tried first; a flue directed the heat from a stove into the neck of a balloon, but only a short flight a few feet up could be achieved in this fashion. Then someone remembered that coal gas, used to light homes and businesses in Richmond, was lighter than air and could be used in a balloon. The gas seemed to work. Now, where to get a balloon?

Dr. Edward Cheves of Savannah, Georgia, a wealthy chemist and inventor, thought balloons had a future in warfare, so he bought up all the silk in Savannah and hired seamstresses to begin the tedious task of sewing the hundreds of thousands of tiny stitches necessary to make tight seams. While this was going on, Dr. Cheves began experimenting to find a varnish that would make the silk impermeable to coal gas. He finally produced such a varnish by melting rubber in oil. On June 24, 1862, the first Confederate balloon arrived in Richmond, and Edward Porter Alexander became the first—and only— "pilot" in the Confederate air force. Alexander would eventually win fame as commander of the Confederate artillery at Gettysburg, but in June 1862, he was still unknown.

Alexander loaded his new balloon on a single railcar towed by a steam engine and rode down to the Richmond Gas Works. Filling his balloon with gas, but keeping it lashed to the railcar, he ordered the train to continue on the tracks until he was close to the fighting front. Then the balloon was untied and up went Alexander, connected to the ground by a single tether rope. On the first few ascents, he could see little, but he signaled his observations to men on the ground, using a wigwag system he had devised. The coal gas had so little lift, however, that full height above the ground could be maintained only for three or four hours before the balloon began to sag toward the earth.

The end for the Confederate air force came on July 4, 1862. The Union army under General George McClellan had begun to retreat from Richmond, and Alexander could no longer reach a good observation point by using the railroad to follow the army. On July 3 his balloon was put aboard a small armed boat, *Teaser,* and towed down the James River to a convenient point. Alexander then went up again. Shortly after sunrise on July 4, the gas began losing its lift so the balloon was reeled in, emptied of gas, and neatly folded. Alexander asked the commander of *Teaser* to run a little farther down the river so he could report to headquarters. *Teaser* headed downriver, but in the process the little boat ran up on a mud bank. The tide would not change for three hours, and while the Teaser was waiting, around a bend in the river came a large Union gunboat, the *Maratanza.*

Quickly, the Confederates set fire to *Teaser* so it would not be captured and, jumping into small boats, rowed for the shore. *Maratanza,* meanwhile, sent her boats to board *Teaser.* The men put out the fire, passed a line to *Maratanza,* pulled *Teaser* free of the mud, and sailed away, balloon and all! This was the end of the Confederate air force. No more balloons were constructed by the South during the entire war.

The U.S. Army abandoned their use of balloons in May 1863. By that time the Confederates had developed the technique of digging a hole into which the trail, or rear support, of a cannon could be placed, causing the muzzle to point sharply skyward. The cannon could then be used to shoot at the U.S. balloons.

The Civil War produced both the first American air forces and the first antiaircraft artillery fire.

THE STORY OF "TAPS"

1862

As any soldier knows, war and romance are contradictory terms. Romance gives one a rose-colored view of life, while war deals with the harshest and most grim realities. Yet for millions of young men across the ages, there has been a certain romantic aura to war. Sometimes elements of military life contribute to that aura. The Civil War brought together thousands of young men who had been brought up in that romantic tradition, who thought of war as a matter of heroic men doing gallant deeds in the name of stainless causes. These young men accepted as part of war grandiose gestures and heroic posturing that today would not only seem out of place but would be laughed at as ridiculous.

But this romantic tradition of war has produced one lasting memento at which no one laughs. This memento is too poignant, too touching, for its appeal to be ignored. It is the bugle call "Taps."

There are many legends about the origins of the call, including the story that it was found on the body of a dead Confederate by his brother who was a Union soldier. The facts are somewhat more prosaic but still interesting.

Daniel Butterfield was born in 1831 in Utica, New York. He was working in New York City as superintendent of the Eastern Division of the American Express Company as the breakup of the nation approached. To prepare himself for war, Butterfield enrolled in the New York militia and eventually became colonel of the twelfth New York Infantry. Marching at its head on May 24, 1861, he led the first Union regiment to cross the Potomac and enter Confederate territory.

Although he had no training in the military, his business experience had taught Butterfield principles of organization that he put to good use on behalf of the army. After preliminary service in and around Martinsburg, Virginia (now West Virginia), where he had a chance to meet the famous Confederate spy Belle Boyd, Butterfield was appointed a brigadier general in a division commanded by General Morrell, a part of Fitz-John Porter's army corps. On June 21, 1862, at the hard-fought battle of Gaines Mill, Butterfield won the Medal of Honor for his bravery under fire.

The Army of the Potomac did not fare well in the battles around Richmond—the Seven Days' Battles—of which Gaines Mill was one. At the beginning of these battles, the Union army was within sight of the church steeples of Richmond. At the conclusion of the battles, the defeated Union soldiers were huddled in camps thirty miles from Richmond, the Confederate capital, contemplating further retreat.

As the Union troops lay in their crowded camps, Butterfield's penchant for organization caused him to search for a solution to a source of confusion. Because spoken commands could not be heard over long distances, orders were transmitted by bugle call. The divisional bugler would sound the call, which would be repeated by the brigade buglers, whose call would in turn be repeated by regimental buglers. But with all the units jammed so close together, how could anyone know which call was meant for whom? Butterfield, who did not read music, had his brigade bugler come up with a three-note recognition signal to precede all calls meant for his units. In a letter written to *Century* magazine in 1898 Butterfield noted,

> *I had composed a call for my brigade, to precede any*
> *calls, indicating that such were calls, or orders, for my*
> *brigade alone. This was of very great use and effect*
> *on the march and in battle. It enabled me to cause*
> *my whole command, at times, in march, covering*
> *over a mile on the road, all to halt instantly, and lie*
> *down. . . . The men rather liked their call, and began*
> *to sing my name to it. It was three notes and a catch. I*
> *can not write a note of music, but have gotten my wife*
> *to write it from my whistling it to her. The men would*
> *sing "Dan, Dan, Dan, Butterfield, Butterfield" to the*
> *notes when a call came. Later, in battle or in some try-*
> *ing circumstance, they sometimes sang "Damn, Damn,*
> *Damn, Butterfield, Butterfield."*

Pleased with this little experiment, Butterfield turned to another matter that annoyed him. To his ears the final bugle call of the day ordering lights out was not very musical. Instead of suggesting the peaceful descent of the end of the day and presenting an invitation to rest, the call was jarring and harsh. Perhaps the general had in his mind the notes of an earlier call, "Tattoo," or perhaps he was working out an original melody. At any rate, because he did not know how to write down musical notes, Butterfield just whistled to himself until he had a tune in mind. Calling in his bugler, Oliver Norton,

Butterfield had the soldier play the call, and the two of them worked out some rough spots. Satisfied, Butterfield ordered the new call to be used in place of the regulation lights out. Bugler Norton said that by the next morning other buglers from other units were coming to ask him for the music to the new call, and he wrote out copies by hand for them. The new call was so much better than the old one that soon it had spread throughout all the Union armies.

The name "Taps" sounds odd when attached to a bugle call, but originally orders for infantry units were sounded on the drum, and a series of taps on a drum was the signal for lights out. When the bugle replaced the drum, the unofficial name for lights out was still applied to the order, and the Butterfield call assumed the name in popular usage.

Shortly after the call was written, Captain John C. Tidball, Battery A, Second Artillery, ordered "Taps" sounded for a funeral. His battery was in an advanced position, and he was afraid that firing the traditional three volleys over the grave of one of his men would cause the Confederates to fire back. The custom of using "Taps" at funerals soon spread throughout the Army of the Potomac, but it did not become the regulation call for that purpose until 1891. There are no official words to the call, but as soon as it was written soldiers began to put words to "Taps," and today there are many popular versions of these words.

There is a stained-glass window in the Old Post Chapel at Fort Monroe that commemorates the sounding of "Taps" at a funeral. The window, dedicated in 1958, shows a bugler and a drummer boy standing beside a flagstaff with the flag at half-staff. There is also a plaque on the grounds of Berkeley Plantation noting that it is the site where the call was written. Butterfield died in 1901. He is buried in an ornate tomb at West Point, despite the fact that he did not attend the academy. There is also a monument to Butterfield near Grant's

Tomb in New York City. Neither of these monuments, nor his biography in the *Dictionary of American Biography,* mentions that he is the author of "Taps." The call was, however, sounded at his funeral.

Daniel Butterfield went on to serve as chief of staff of the Army of the Potomac and the Army of the Cumberland. He retired as a major general in the regular army and went on to hold numerous important political and business posts before his death. Today all of that is forgotten, and very few Americans even recognize his name. But all over the world people know "Taps."

THE STRANGER

1862

Memorial Day in the town of Gray, Maine, located near the larger city of Freeport, is celebrated in a special way. As in many small towns, the day is the occasion for a parade, with local groups marching down the streets, many waving flags, to honor the veterans of past wars. In Gray, once the parade reaches its official end, a small honor guard breaks away from the crowd and enters the town cemetery. There, small U.S. flags already fly over the graves of American soldiers, but the honor guard has come to visit the as yet unmarked grave of another American soldier. Reaching a plot bearing a small stone engraved with the word STRANGER, the honor guard pauses and with a degree of ceremony plants an American flag—not the Stars and Stripes, but the Stars and Bars. How this unknown Confederate came to lie in the soil of Maine, and how he comes to be remembered on Memorial Day is a fascinating story.

On August 9, 1862, the preliminary maneuvering for the Second Manassas campaign was under way. The Second Army

Corps of the Army of Northern Virginia, led by General Thomas Jonathan "Stonewall" Jackson, was moving northward against the Army of Virginia led by General John Pope. Pope had been brought from the Western theater, where he had won a significant victory at Island No. 10 near New Madrid, Missouri. In doing so, the Union army had captured a Confederate stronghold on the Mississippi River, allowing an advance on Memphis, Tennessee. On arriving in Virginia, Pope had become controversial for adopting a harsh policy toward Confederate civilians behind his lines. He also had made himself appear faintly ridiculous by issuing orders as coming from "Head Quarters in the Saddle," leading wags to comment that "Pope had his head quarters where his hind quarters belonged." The Confederate forces, anxious to "suppress that man," as Robert E. Lee put it, were out for revenge against Pope.

Among the troops under Pope's command was a brigade of rookie soldiers commanded by General Samuel W. Crawford, a former surgeon who had been part of the garrison of Fort Sumter when the war began. One regiment of Crawford's Brigade was the Tenth Maine Infantry, in which served Lieutenant Charles H. Colley of Gray, Maine. These men had not seen battle before, but they were eager for a chance to prove themselves against the veteran Southern troops awaiting them.

The first week of August 1862 had been a scorcher. Each day, the temperature had risen into the eighties as soon as the sun came up and rose well into the nineties during the afternoon. A coating of dust lay thick on all the roads and fields, and foliage drooped in the copses of woods, so there was scant shade for relief from the blistering heat. One member of the Tenth Maine remembered that the air had been quite hot even when the men were lying still, and that he could not imagine how hot it would be when the regiment was given the order to march.

That order soon came because the Blue and Gray were slogging along the dusty roads of Virginia and were about to engage in combat along the slopes and fields surrounding a gentle hill called Cedar Mountain. Ominously, the hill was sometimes called Slaughter Mountain. Moving into position on the Union right flank, General Crawford took post along the edge of a wheat field. From his lines the field sloped down, then rose to a crest, then sloped down again to a woods held by the Confederates.

Crawford surveyed the situation and, believing the woods to be only lightly held, ordered his brigade into formation for a charge. Just as the men were on the verge of attack, the Tenth Maine was ordered to hold back in order to support a battery of artillery located nearby. Across the wheat field the brigade charged, and the Confederate lines broke. Some fifteen minutes after the Union force disappeared into the woods in pursuit of the rebels, the Tenth Maine was ordered forward. But the tide of battle turned again as Confederate reinforcements met Crawford head on and turned his troops back. The Tenth Maine had just reached the crest in the middle of the field when their friends came swarming back toward their original position. The Tenth found itself all alone trying to stem the tide as Confederates closed in. For five to ten terrible minutes, the regiment stood its ground, silhouetted against the sky, and was ripped to pieces by gunfire, losing half of its men. One of the men in the regiment described the sharp "zip" of the minié balls that tore past the ears of the boys from Maine and how that sound was joined by a new noise as additional Confederates came against them. The new noise was the softer singing made by weapons loaded with "buck and ball," a cartridge containing a round musket ball and three buckshot. At close ranges the buck-and-ball load was deadlier than the more famous minié ball. Soldiers often spoke of bullets flying past them in sheets or spattering the ground like hail. The Tenth was in just such a predicament as they stood on the crest of the slight ridge with nothing more substantial for protection than an occasional shock of wheat. In a few minutes the Tenth Maine lost 24 killed and 175 wounded, including Lieutenant Charles Colley.

At last the field grew quiet. At dusk a truce was arranged to remove the wounded of both sides. Among those carried off the field was Lieutenant Colley. Although he was taken to a hospital at Alexandria, Virginia, where he could receive the best treatment possible, his wounds proved mortal, and Lieutenant Colley died a few days later.

When word arrived of the death of their son, Amos and Sarah Colley went to considerable effort and expense to have his body embalmed and shipped home for burial. On the sad day when the coffin arrived, Mrs. Colley insisted that it be opened so she could see her son's face one last time. When the coffin was opened, Sarah Colley gave a shriek of horror and disbelief. The body was not that of her son! Not only was the corpse that of a stranger, it was dressed in a Confederate uniform.

Once the initial shock had worn off, the Colleys realized that they were now dependent on the kindness of strangers for the proper burial of their son; therefore, they would show kindness and respect to this son of strangers. The body of the unknown Confederate was taken to the village cemetery and there interred. Following the war, money was collected locally and a small stone memorial erected on which were engraved the words, STRANGER. A SOLDIER OF THE LATE WAR, DIED 1862.

A few weeks after the funeral for the Confederate stranger, the body of Lieutenant Colley was found and returned to his parents. Colley was buried near the rebel soldier, and to this day the two former enemies lie only a few feet apart, both resting in eternal peace. And every Memorial Day, the citizens of Gray, Maine, remember their Stranger.

Author's note: One Confederate regiment that inflicted such great casualities on the Tenth Maine was the First Tennessee in which my great-great-grandfather fought as a private. One cannot help wondering, did he fire the shot that mortally wounded Lieutenant Colley?

FROM MALTA TO SOUTH
MOUNTAIN, MARYLAND

1862

The American Civil War was, in many ways, a magnet drawing to itself adventurers and patriots from around the globe. Thousands of immigrants from Ireland, Germany, and other European countries got off the boats and soon took their places in the ranks of fighting men, most of them in the North. One of the most famous brigades of the Army of the Potomac was the Irish Brigade, which fought under a green flag emblazoned with a golden harp. Entire units of the Union army obeyed commands uttered in German, and if asked about their military organization would reply in broken English, "I fights mit Siegel." Franz Siegel was one of the most famous of the German revolutionary leaders who had come to the United States following the failed liberal revolution of 1848.

The Confederacy had its share of foreign-born troops and leaders, too, from the Irish-born Patrick Cleburne and the "Fighting Sons of Erin" of the Tenth Tennessee to Hispanic units from Texas and adventurers such as Heros von Borcke, who served on the staff of Confederate General James E. B. (Jeb) Stuart.

Perhaps the most unusual of all foreign-born soldiers was Orlando Caruana, who was born at Ca Valletta on the Mediterranean island of Malta, and who would win the Medal of Honor on the slopes of South Mountain, Maryland, on September 14, 1862.

Caruana, like all boys on Malta, grew up knowing something of the sea and was from a family with a long tradition of seafaring and trading. Not wishing to be a sailor or a ship's officer, Caruana was trained as a clerk or bookkeeper. In this capacity he traveled all over the Mediterranean and Europe as well as making several voyages to America. In the summer of 1861, his ship made harbor at New York City. Recruiters for various units were stirring up enthusiasm for enlistment and offering cash incentives. Ready for a change of scene, Caruana enlisted in Company K, Fifty-first New York Infantry. His clerical skills were useful in his new occupation, and he soon rose to the rank of sergeant.

In the early autumn of 1862, Robert E. Lee had led the Army of Northern Virginia into Maryland in the first Confederate offensive outside of Virginia. While elements of his army were camped around Frederick, Maryland, a copy of Lee's orders for future movements was lost, only to be discovered by Union soldiers. Taking advantage of this information, George McClellan led the Army of the Potomac in pursuit of the Confederates. The first contact between the armies would come along the slopes of South Mountain.

Stretching across the narrow waist of western Maryland from north to south, the ridge of South Mountain is part of the larger Blue Ridge chain, which extends down into Virginia and up into Pennsylvania. About 1,200 feet in elevation, the steep slopes of the ridge provide good military positions from which to delay any pursuit. Somewhere up there the rebels were waiting. The Union cavalry couldn't tell where the Southern boys were because the mountain was covered with thickets of mountain laurel and scrub oak. Here and there, open fields and pastures interrupted the tangle of vegetation, but both sides tried to stay out of the open areas. In the brush a person was at least hidden, while a soldier crossing an opening would be an easy prey to an enemy hidden on the other side.

General McClellan was not moving rapidly that morning of September 14. Lee's "Lost Order" detailing Confederate plans had been handed to him the day before. Though he should have acted quickly, McClellan had spent several hours planning his moves and drafting orders for his various units. The unit commanders didn't begin marching until the next morning.

The Second Division under General Samuel Sturgis did not get its orders to march from corps commander Jesse L. Reno until one o'clock in the afternoon on September 14. The Second Brigade of that division, commanded by General Edward Ferrero, including Orlando Caruana's Fifty-first New York, were even later taking the road. Major General Reno, commanding the IX Army Corps, was ordered to follow the National Road through Turner's Gap in his advance against the enemy.

As Ferrero's brigade neared South Mountain, the smoke of battle could already be seen on the slopes ahead. One unit of the IX Corps, the division of General Jacob Cox, had moved out early that morning. That division had gone to the left, to the south of the National Road, in an attempt to turn the right flank of the Confederate position. It had been successful, but fresh Southern troops had fought the division to a standstill before it could carry Turner's Gap.

About four o'clock that afternoon, Ferrero's Second Brigade reached the center of the developing battlefield. Colonel Robert Potter of the Fifty-first New York called for volunteers to scout ahead to find the enemy lines. Sergeant Orlando Caruana and three privates stepped forward.

As silently as possible, the four men crept through the thickets. A hundred yards behind them came a long, thin skirmish line of Yankees. Farther behind them, in turn, came the complete battle line of Ferrero's brigade. After a time the four advance scouts reached a fence and halted, looking at a large, cleared field. They paused to allow the skirmish line to catch up, then the officer commanding the skirmishers decided to wait for the battle line to come up and consolidate the position before continuing.

As the soldiers in blue took their places behind the fence, General Reno, IX Corps commander, rode up. Seeing the sweaty, tired men, Reno told them to rest and to make coffee; the advance would resume in a few minutes. As their comrades rested and collected sticks for small fires, Caruana and his companions crossed the field and entered the far woods. They had gone only a short way when they saw a sight that brought their hearts into their mouths. Advancing directly toward them in battle line was an entire division of Confederate troops. Their flags identified them as the elite force commanded by General John B. Hood.

There was no time for stealth. Caruana and the others turned and began to run as fast as the mountain terrain would allow. Their sudden movement caught the attention of the Confederate skirmishers, and the chase was on. Minié balls whizzed past Caruana's ears, clipping twigs from the branches around him. One after the other, his companions went down, dead or mortally wounded. Panting and gasping, Caruana reached the field only to see, with dismay, that his regiment and the Fifty-first Pennsylvania were milling around in the open space. Yelling to alert the men of the impending attack, Caruana was speeding toward General Reno when a volcano blast of fire swept the field. Reno fell dead and the lines of the Fifty-first

New York and the Fifty-first Pennsylvania were shattered. To make matters worse, other Union regiments began firing at friend and foe alike.

The Fifty-first New York would see much more hard fighting before September 14 came to an end. They would see harder still at Burnside's Bridge over Antietam Creek three days later. But the memory of Sergeant Orlando Caruana's brave act on behalf of his adopted country was not forgotten.

In 1890 ex-Colonel Robert Potter, now an old man, submitted a recommendation that former Sergeant Caruana be awarded for his bravery and sacrifice with the Medal of Honor. Congress agreed, and twenty-eight years after the fact, Orlando Caruana received recognition for his bravery. Recognition was delayed, but not denied.

Author's note: The most extreme example of delayed recognition is the case of Sergeant Andrew Jackson Smith of the Fifty-fifth Massachusetts, an African-American regiment. In 1864, in an engagement at Ridgeland, South Carolina, Sergeant Smith picked up his regiment's fallen flag and carried the banner for the rest of the battle. His act of heroism resulted in his being recommended for the Medal of Honor fifty-three years later in 1917. The medal was awarded to his descendent, Mr. Andrew Bowman of Indianapolis, Indiana, on January 16, 2001.

THE BATTLE CAUSED
BY THREE CIGARS

1862

At nightfall on September 17, 1862, more than twenty-three thousand young Americans from the North and the South lay bleeding and dying on the hills overlooking Antietam Creek, near the little Maryland town of Sharpsburg. In a way, they had been brought to their fate by three cigars. The battle, brought on by a chance discovery, was to have far-reaching implications for the future of the United States. Although the fighting ended in a tactical draw, President Abraham Lincoln would use the event to announce that he would issue an Emancipation Proclamation, to go into effect on January 1, 1863, about ninety days after the battle at Sharpsburg. The proclamation would be a curious document; it declared freedom for the slaves behind Confederate lines, where Lincoln had no control, and left in slavery those behind Union lines, where Lincoln did have control. However, the battle of Antietam, also called the battle of Sharpsburg, gave President Lincoln his opportunity to change the nature of the war by implying that the end of slavery would be a war aim of the Union.

There had already been plenty of fighting and dying in 1862 before the war had moved from Virginia to Maryland. In late June and early July, the Confederate army defending Richmond, the Confederate capital, had fought a series of battles under its new commander, General Robert E. Lee. These battles, called the Seven Days' Battles, forced the Union army, commanded by General George McClellan, to give up its attempt to capture Richmond and to retreat. Lee then led his army against McClellan's replacement, General John Pope, and completely smashed Pope's army in the battle of Second Manassas. Now as Lee's Army of Northern Virginia moved across the Potomac River into Maryland, there were lots of people, North and South, who would have agreed that enough young men had been shot for one year, but there were soon to be more.

The Confederate objectives in moving north were quite simple. The Southerners wanted to live off the Maryland countryside and give the farmers in Virginia a chance to harvest their crops untroubled by the war. In this they were successful in a limited way. About all the Maryland countryside had to offer was half-ripe apples and green corn, both of which made a definite impact on one's digestion when eaten regularly in large quantities. A second objective was to find wearing apparel. The Confederates had been fighting and marching almost continuously for more than ten weeks. Uniforms had become dirt-stained and ragged, while shoes had completely disintegrated. Lee's own estimate was that several thousand of his men were barefoot. By moving into Maryland, there was a chance to find shoes and to acquire clothing.

After a few days of moving lazily through the rolling hills of Maryland near the town of Frederick, Lee made a command decision. He would divide his army into three parts, sending two of them south to capture the Union-held town of Harpers Ferry, Virginia (now West Virginia). This capture would open a supply line, allowing the Army of Northern Virginia to receive flour, meat, and ammunition from the Shenandoah Valley of Virginia. Orders to accomplish this goal were drawn up, and copies were sent to every general commanding a division in Lee's army. On September 10 the Army of Northern Virginia split up, with each segment moving off to accomplish its separate goal. The separate pieces of the army were to reunite by September 15.

About noon on September 13, units of the Union Army of the Potomac, again commanded by General McClellan, moved into Frederick following the Confederates. Up to this point Union objectives had been very simple. McClellan was waiting to see what Lee would do and then McClellan would react. There were no definite plans. Good camping places for large numbers of men were hard to find, so in many cases the boys in blue occupied the same spots recently evacuated by the boys in gray. That was why Private Barton Mitchell, Company E of the Twenty-seventh Indiana Infantry, was not particularly surprised when he saw a bulky envelope lying in the grass where he had just dropped down to rest after a morning marching. There was a certain amount of trash and clutter lying about, left by the Confederates. Interrupting his chat with his buddy, Sergeant John Bloss, Mitchell reached over and picked up the envelope. It was not sealed and inside was a sheet of paper wrapped around three cigars.

Soldiers in the Civil War were not paid a lot of money, and good cigars were a little costly, so the two men felt they had found a real treat. But just as they prepared to light up, Mitchell looked at the paper. Handwritten, it was covered with names everyone knew from the newspapers: James Longstreet, Thomas "Stonewall"

Jackson, D. H. Hill, Robert E. Lee. Here was a copy of Lee's official orders! This was more important than a good smoke. The men took their discovery to their company commander, a Captain Koop, and from there they were sent to the regimental commander, Colonel Silas Colgrove.

Within a short time George McClellan had the paper on the table in front of him in his tent. There, before his eyes, was a complete copy of Lee's plans. McClellan knew not only that the Confederate army was scattered, he knew where each piece of it was, what that piece was supposed to do, and when they were supposed to do it. McClellan was, understandably, overjoyed. To a friend he remarked, "Here is a paper with which, if I cannot whip Bobbie Lee, I will be willing to go home." Then he added that the army would move *tomorrow*. This one word betrayed the flaw in McClellan's character. He was overly cautious. With the plans of the opposing army in his hands and with several hours of daylight left, McClellan wanted to wait until "tomorrow" to move. Already the window of golden opportunity was closing. Lee's order called for the Army of Northern Virginia to reunite by September 15, and it was already September 13. If ever bold, swift action was called for, now was the time. The South's largest army and its most prestigious general could be destroyed, but only if McClellan acted at once.

With the paper, McClellan indeed should have been able to whip Lee, especially because Lee's men had not been able to keep to his deadlines and were behind schedule. But McClellan was his own worst enemy. His cautious nature slowed his movements; he overestimated the strength of the Confederate army; and he allowed hard-fighting Confederates to hold him back. It was not until September 17 that he attacked Lee's army in what became known as the battle of Antietam, one of the bloodiest battles of the Civil War. By that time

Lee had brought most of his men back together, although some of them came up at the last minute, literally on the dead run. Ironically, there is no record of what happened to the three cigars whose discovery so changed the course of the Civil War and of American history.

McClellan lost his big chance to "whip Bobbie Lee," and he did get sent home for the rest of the war. With him went over twenty-three thousand young Americans, including Private Mitchell, who became one of the casualties of the battle he had helped to bring about, a battle sparked by three cigars.

THE ANGEL OF MARYE'S HEIGHTS

1862

Sergeant Richard Kirkland could hear the moaning of the wounded as he stood behind the stone wall. "Water, water," they cried. Cold as it was, they still craved water.

Cautiously, Kirkland raised his head just enough for his eyes to clear the wall. There were Yankee sharpshooters out there who would be happy enough to put a bullet through his head, get a little revenge for what the rebels had done to them the day before, December 13, 1862.

The scene that met Kirkland's gaze was one of human wreckage. The ground sloped gently down across broad, bare fields to a canal about four hundred yards away. Yesterday the Union Army of the Potomac had marched out of the little town of Fredericksburg, crossed the canal, and formed lines of battle. The Southern artillery on Marye's Heights, behind Kirkland, had pounded the blue columns unmercifully as they marched. Once the battle lines had formed and the blue wave rolled forward, it was time for the riflemen to join in. Sheets of lead, tongues of fire, had poured across the top of the stone wall from where Kirkland and his comrades had stood in ranks four and five deep. He had lost count of the number of times the blue wave had rolled forward (brave men, even if they were on the enemy side), but their efforts had not mattered; none of them had even gotten close to the stone wall. By the end of the day, the field was a solid carpet of blue, many of the men still in death, but many, many more writhing in agony from their wounds. More of them were still this morning. The freezing temperatures of the night before had carried off hundreds, but still hundreds more remained alive. Their commander, General Ambrose Burnside, was too proud to ask for a truce; he would let his men die miserable deaths in the frozen mud rather than admit he was beaten.

A rifle cracked and a minié ball whizzed close past Kirkland's head. "Dang," he thought, ducking, "a man can still get killed out here. But I can't stand this moaning. I've got to do something to help those wounded men; I don't care if they are Yankees."

Sergeant Kirkland went to his commanding officer, Colonel John Kennedy, Second South Carolina Infantry. Colonel Kennedy could see and hear the wounded as well as Kirkland, but he could also see the occasional burst of a shell sent over by the Yankee artillery and could hear the "zip, zip" of rifle bullets cutting past his ear when he looked over the wall. Sergeant Kirkland asked to be allowed to go over the wall and assist the wounded. Kennedy replied:

> *Sergeant, I feel sorry for those boys lying out there. They never had a chance. I heard General Longstreet tell General Lee that if they gave us enough ammunition we could kill every Yankee on the planet before they reached this wall, and he was right. I'd like to help those poor fellows, but there is no truce between the*

armies. Every time we show ourselves, we get shot at. I have as much human sympathy as anyone else, but my first responsibility is to save the lives of my own men. I can't let you go out there, sergeant. Permission denied.

So Kirkland returned to his post, but the cries of the wounded still stirred his heart. In the afternoon he went back to see Colonel Kennedy and got permission to go speak to his brigade commander, General Joseph Kershaw. Although he respected his general, Kirkland was not exactly in awe of him; he had known General Kershaw all his life. Back home in Camden, South Carolina, the Kirklands and the Kershaws were neighbors; Richard's father was a friend of General Kershaw, and the general had been a guest in the Kirkland home on many occasions. But that didn't mean General Kershaw would approve the sergeant's request.

"Sorry, sergeant. I cannot permit it. You would be riddled with bullets the minute you stepped over the wall. I can't let you go. If I let you get killed like that, what would I tell your mother and father?"

"General, sir, my parents approve of my being here fighting to protect my home. I think they would approve even more if I tried to save life now that the fighting has stopped."

"Son, you are making this hard for me. How do you propose to do this?"

"General, I'll gather canteens from my buddies and carry as much water as I can. I'll stick both hands up over the wall so they can see I don't have a gun and then, real slow, I'll climb over and go to the closest wounded man. Maybe one of my buddies can wave a white flag when I start as a signal I'm coming to save life."

"Sergeant, if you are bound and determined to go, then go. But I cannot allow a white flag. An officer in the Union lines might mistake that for a signal for a general truce, and since there is no such truce, I could get into big trouble. No flag. But, God bless you, Richard."

"Thank you, sir."

Back at his post it took only a few minutes for Richard to collect all the canteens he could carry. Nervously, cautiously, he raised both hands above the wall, and slowly he stood up. All his friends held their breath. Each second could be Richard's last if the Yankees misunderstood what he was doing and shot at him.

Silence covered that part of the battlefield. Richard walked quickly to the nearest wounded Union soldier. Gently, he raised the man's head, gave him a drink of water, and unbuckled the man's blanket from his knapsack and wrapped him in it. For more than ninety minutes, Richard did what he could for the wounded in front of his regiment, making several trips to a nearby well to refill his canteens. He stopped his work only when it was too dark to see.

As he crossed the stone wall back to his friends, Sergeant Richard Kirkland knew he had just done the best work he had ever accomplished in all his life. This veteran soldier was nineteen years old.

The Confederate army did not give medals for bravery, but Sergeant Kirkland was rewarded with a two-month leave to visit his parents and home community. In May 1863 he fought in the battle of Chancellorsville and at Salem Church. In July, on the second day of the battle of Gettysburg, Richard Kirkland fought so bravely and well that he was promoted to lieutenant. Two months later he fought, with the rest of his brigade, at Chickamauga in northern Georgia. While taking part in an attack on the retreating Union forces, Richard was shot in the chest. With his last breath he said, "Tell Father I died right."

Today in the Quaker Cemetery in Camden, South Carolina, there stands a modest stone inscribed:

RICHARD KIRKLAND

DIED DEFENDING HIS COUNTRY

1843–1863

In the National Battlefield Park at Fredericksburg, Virginia, in front of the part of the stone wall held by the Second South Carolina during the battle, there is a larger-than-life statue of a soldier stooping to help a wounded man. Its inscription says:

SERGEANT RICHARD KIRKLAND

C.S.A.

THE ANGEL OF MARYE'S HEIGHTS

DECEMBER 14, 1862

THE FEMALE MOSES—
HARRIET TUBMAN

1863

The American Civil War became the stuff of legends even as it was being fought. Passions were high on both sides, and propaganda was produced in copious amounts, always depicting one side as great and good, while the other side was presented as petty and evil. Further, slow communication of news made it more likely that credence would be given to rumors that created larger-than-life individuals whose exploits and heroism were superhuman. Somewhere at the heart of these exaggerations, there was usually a real person, but in many cases that person was obscured by the mists of folklore. Such a person is Harriet Tubman, the Moses of her people.

Much of the folklore about Harriet Tubman came from abolitionist writings published just before the Civil War. An attempt was made to create pure antislavery heroes who combated evil slaveholders. These stories were added to when a book was published by some of Harriet's close friends in the days immediately after the war. At that time Harriet was in danger of losing her home because of an unpaid mortgage, and the book was written to be a best seller, appealing to an audience exhilarated by the end of the struggle. (Incidentally, the mortgage had not been paid because Harriet Tubman had been working for the United States government for three years without pay.)

Harriet was born a slave about 1820 in the Eastern Shore district of Maryland. At age five she was hired out to a neighboring family who didn't have slaves, and when she was seven years old, she was assigned to take care of a white infant. At such a young age, she was incapable of doing that job well and was often punished for inattention to duty. As Harriet grew older, she developed unusual physical strength and came to prefer outdoor work, although working in the house was less demanding. At age twenty-nine Harriet became the wife of a free black man, and though a slave herself, she was allowed to stay with him each night. By this time Harriet had a strong desire to be free, but her husband does not appear to have shared this dream. In fact, when the topic was raised, he discouraged her from attempting to go north.

Harriet was anything but a docile slave. Like many slaves who were hired out, she was required to pay her owner an annual fee, but she could keep any money earned over and above this amount. Having accumulated a small sum, one night Harriet simply left her husband and started on her own for Philadelphia. She made it to free territory, and soon she was earning her living as a free woman in Philadelphia. Although she seems to have had no desire to be reunited with her husband, Harriet did want to bring her family out of Maryland, where they were slaves, to the North and freedom. Forays into the South to gather up slaves and help them escape were frowned on by antislavery forces, but Harriet made at least three trips between 1850 and 1857 to help family members and other people escape.

The growing abolitionist movement was looking for people to help promote and popularize its cause. Harriet was illiterate but articulate, and hers was an interesting story. Soon she was a regular feature at abolitionist meetings, where she became well known as a symbol of what the movement was trying to accomplish. In 1857 William Seward, later a leading member of Congress, secretary of state, and famous for Seward's Folly—the purchase of Alaska—sold Harriet a house in Auburn, New York. This building, still standing, would be her home for fifty years.

The real contribution of Harriet Tubman came when the Civil War began. One of the first Union successes came on the coast of Georgia and South Carolina, where islands were occupied by Federal troops. Numbers of escaped slaves flocked to the islands, and in both South Carolina and Massachusetts, African Americans were being recruited into the Union army. Disease and injury were soon rampant among these enlistees, so the governor of Massachusetts asked Harriet to go to Port Royal, South Carolina, to assist in caring for those in hospitals there and rally those who wanted to join the Union lines. In March 1862, Harriet went. At the time, ending slavery was not an objective of the Union cause, but Harriet's reputation as a symbol of abolition led many to begin thinking that it should be.

Medical care was crude at best during the Civil War, and nursing was not the skilled occupation it is today, but Harriet was determined to do her best. Much to her surprise, Harriet found herself facing a language barrier. Most of the local African Americans spoke Gullah, a dialect that contained numerous West African words. And there was the question of how she would support herself because she was not being paid to nurse soldiers. She baked and sold pies to earn money. She was working for freedom but was receiving less in the way of support than she had when she was a slave.

Harriet described her hospital work in this way:

I'd go to the hospital, I would, every morning. I'd get a big chunk of ice and put it in a basin and fill it with water; then I'd take a sponge and begin. First man I'd come to I'd shoo away the flies and they'd rise like bees around a hive. Then I'd begin to bathe their wounds and by the time I'd bathed three or four or five the fire and the heat would have melted the ice and it would be red as clear blood. Then I'd get more ice and by the time I got to the next ones the flies would be swarming around the first ones as black and thick as ever.

On at least one occasion—in June 1863—Harriet accompanied a military force aboard several gunboats and steamers up the Combahee River. This expedition destroyed a good deal of cotton and burned numerous houses while escorting 756 slaves to freedom. Anxious that it should be widely known that these slaves had been freed by African-American soldiers, Harriet had a letter sent to Frank Sanborn, a leading abolitionist, confident he would have the letter printed in papers. She said, "Don't you think we colored people are entitled for some of the credit of that exploit? We weakened the rebels . . . by bringing away seven hundred and fifty-six 'contrabands.' Of those seven hundred and fifty-six nearly or quite all the able-bodied men have joined the colored regiments here."

Although her legend has Harriet Tubman stalking through swamps as a spy or using a pistol to ward off those trying to catch fugitive slaves, the real Harriet is a more admirable person, a woman willing to do hard, boring work with no pay while using all her talents in the interest of putting an end to slavery. Even without the legends, she was indeed a Moses for her people.

HIS COUNTRY'S HIGHEST
AWARD FOR BRAVERY

1863

Daylight came slowly, grudgingly, over the torn cedar thickets and ravished farm fields on the banks of Stones River. As the light slowly increased and solid forms resolved themselves out of shadows, thousands of soldiers in blue and in gray peered toward where the enemy lines had been last night when darkness fell. Thousands more stared upward toward the sky with eyes dimmed with pain or vacant in death. The Grim Reaper had enjoyed high carnival on the last day of the old year.

Now it was New Year's Day, 1863, and many were wondering what the new year would bring to their countries and their families, and if they would live to see the end of the year.

The Eighth Tennessee Volunteer Infantry, about three hundred strong this morning, were among those wondering. They all knew that on this particular morning a milestone in history was being passed. On this day the Emancipation Proclamation was going into effect, and all slaves behind Southern lines were declared free.

Curiously enough, slaves behind Northern lines were still slaves. But national politics was not the most pressing issue on the minds of the men of the Eighth Tennessee.

Across a cotton field, perhaps four hundred yards away, the soldiers of the Eighth could clearly see the Union line of infantry and artillery. All day yesterday the Eighth had helped to shove that line back. It had not been easy, and almost two hundred men from the Eighth had gone down, dead or wounded, in accomplishing that task. But now, as they peered out from the trees of one of the thickets that dotted the battlefield, the men were preparing to make one more push.

The Union line at which the Eighth was looking was literally standing in the Nashville Pike. Only fifty or so yards away was the Nashville and Chattanooga Railroad. Push the Yankees back from there and the Union Army of the Cumberland would be destroyed. Many would be killed and captured and the rest would be reduced to disorganized fragments of units before they could make their way back to Nashville. Corporal George Dance of the Eighth could just imagine the headlines in the next day's papers: "Emancipation Proclamation in Effect, Union Army Destroyed, Rebels March on Cincinnati."

But that would not happen easily. Those Yankees over yonder across the cotton field were tough soldiers—men from Ohio, Illinois, Indiana, and Michigan. They were hard fighters whom the Eighth had faced on other fields, and all those fields had been the sites of fierce battles.

George Dance was a big man. He stood about six feet, three inches in an army whose average soldier stood five feet, seven inches. And at 175 pounds he outweighed most of his comrades by forty pounds or more. George was a farmer from Lincoln County, Tennessee, a county named for a general in the first War for Independence.

George had joined the Eighth Tennessee in 1861, when this war for independence had just begun, and he had served faithfully and well in every battle and skirmish his regiment had been in. He had served so well he had been promoted twice.

After the regiment's first big battle at Shiloh, George had been asked to serve in the color guard. That was quite an honor, albeit a dangerous one. A regiment's flag was not only a symbol of pride and honor, it was the focal point of a unit in battle. When the noise of battle made it impossible to hear orders, soldiers followed the flag. As men went down, the gaps were filled by closing in on the colors. The taller the men who carried the flag, the better the emblem could be seen. But the flag was also the object of intense gunfire from the enemy and was the objective of counterattacks. The color guard was to keep the flag flying at all times. If the flag bearer went down, another member of the guard was to pick up the banner immediately. The members of the color guard were not even to fire their guns unless it appeared the flag was in danger of capture.

George had been in the color guard of the Eighth at Perryville, Kentucky, and had been promoted in rank from private to corporal because of his bravery on that field. Now he was outwardly calm but inwardly apprehensive. George Dance knew what awaited him once the attack started.

All along the battle line, the Confederate Army of Tennessee was stirring. Regiments were falling into ranks and assembling in their brigade formations. Already the artillery on each side was firing, trying to knock out the opposing cannon. As soon as the Confederate infantry broke from the woods, George Dance knew the Union artillery would ignore the Confederate guns and concentrate their fire on the foot soldiers. At least it would be quick. With a fairly short advance, they would either break the Union line, or they would be repulsed in only a few minutes. Bloody but swift would be the nature of this fight.

The infantry was in place now. Their artillery fell quiet. Then there was the order, "Forward, march!" Only a few steps and they were in the open. Immediately, men began to fall as shells burst over their line. "Steady! Steady! Close up on the colors!" George could hear the officers calling.

This was bad. Shiloh had been fought in the woods where there was some protection. At Perryville, the Eighth had been on the defensive part of the time. But this was hellish. No protection at all, just cotton stalks less than knee high. Now they were only about three hundred yards away from the Union lines, and there came the sound George and every other soldier dreaded, the sharp crackle of rifle fire—the voice of the deadliest weapon of the war.

All around him George could hear the shriek of artillery shells and the zip of rifle bullets. All around him his comrades were going down, some with a scream, some in silence. Then he saw it. The flag was down. The color sergeant had been hit three times at once and was dead before his body hit the ground. With no thought or hesitation, George Dance picked up the flag and led the steady advance of the Eighth Tennessee.

There was Colonel John Moore. What was he saying? "Fall back, men. Fall ba . . ." The colonel went down, mortally wounded. Like any sensible man, George was afraid, but he was more afraid of being thought a coward than of death, so he walked off the field backward. If he was shot, he wanted it to be in the front, not in the back.

Once he arrived under the cover of the woods, it was better. More cover meant fewer bullets whistling by. But there were not many men left in the Eighth Tennessee. Of the three hundred who had started across the cotton field, fewer than half were still on their feet. If the Union army were to be pushed back, somebody else would have to do it.

In the end the Union army was not pushed back. On the night of January 3, 1863, George Dance was called to regimental head-quarters. The major in temporary command of the unit returned his salute.

"Corporal Dance, we are sending the body of Colonel Moore back to his home for burial. The army is retreating in that direction. You will accompany the burial detail, and then you will have a furlough of thirty days. You have a wife and children, I believe."

"Yes, sir, major."

"Well, when you arrive home, tell them this. Our army gives no medals for bravery, but to those who are the bravest of the brave, we give furloughs and promotions. It is my pleasure and honor to name you color sergeant of the Eighth Tennessee."

George Dance returned to his unit after his furlough and served the rest of the war as its color sergeant. He carried the flag of his regiment through some of the worst carnage of the conflict. In 1912 the survivors of the Eighth Tennessee gathered for a reunion. In the picture made at that reunion, George Dance stands in the proper place for the color sergeant, at the extreme left flank of the line. He is not stooped with age, although his hair and moustache are snow white against his black skin. Color Sergeant George Dance, Eighth Tennessee, CSA, was a valiant African-American soldier. He won his country's highest award for bravery.

LOYAL SERVANT—
VALIANT SERGEANT

1863

"Mother, most of the servants have left the army and have gone back to their homes since we returned from Kentucky. I would like for George to come up here to Murfreesboro to do the washing and cooking for my mess, if you can spare him. But I only want him to come if he wants to." So wrote Captain Robert Singleton from the encampment of the Confederate army around Murfreesboro to his mother at Fairfield, Tennessee, in the late autumn of 1862.

The Singletons were not wealthy plantation owners with large numbers of slaves, but they did own an above-average-size farm and held half a dozen slaves. When the Civil War began, Robert, the oldest son, joined the Seventeenth Tennessee Infantry and soon rose to the rank of captain. He fought at Shiloh in April 1862 and at Perryville, Kentucky, in October. Now he was back in Tennessee and was asking his mother to send one of the family slaves, George, to be his body servant, "if he wants to" come.

Robert and George were the same age and had spent a good deal of time as boyhood companions doing what boys of that era did in the country—playing in the creek, throwing rocks, fishing, hunting, watching hawks circle overhead. On a farm like the one the Singletons owned, no one was idle, so both boys worked at jobs appropriate to their age and strength. Despite the differences of race and status, a degree of respect, if not friendship, grew between them, as evidenced by Robert asking if George wanted to come instead of ordering his presence in the camp.

George traveled to meet up with Robert and spent a few weeks in the Confederate camp in Murfreesboro doing the necessary tasks involved in being the servant of an officer's mess, but battle was imminent. On December 31, 1862, the Confederates surprised the opposing Union force and rolled the blue line back toward the Nashville Pike, the Union's only line of retreat. Thousands fell in the terrific struggle, among them Captain Robert Singleton, struck in the right thigh by a minié ball. Carried to a field hospital, Robert was told his leg required amputation.

When Robert regained consciousness from the chloroform, his right leg was gone, but George was there, sitting by his cot. All night George did what he could to relieve Robert's suffering, but by morning he knew hands more skillful and tender than his were needed. Taking Robert's horse, George rode almost thirty miles to Fairfield and told Mrs. Singleton of her son's wound. A short time later a wagon driven by George and carrying Mrs. Singleton left for Murfreesboro.

Carefully, as only a mother could, Mrs. Singleton, aided by George, nursed Robert. Even when the Confederates retreated and Robert's hospital was taken over by the Union army, they stayed. Gradually, Robert's wound healed and strength slowly returned to his body. One day a Union officer announced that despite his disabling wound, Robert would be sent to a prisoner of war camp at Fort Delaware. The death rate at Fort Delaware was quite high even for healthy prisoners, so Mrs. Singleton and George said their good-byes with the fear they would never see Robert again.

The wagon rolled back to Fairfield, again driven by George and carrying Mrs. Singleton. For George, the emotional stress of this return journey must have been even greater than that of the grieving mother. Within Union lines in Murfreesboro, George had been a free man; in Fairfield he was a slave. One can only wonder at the sense of loyalty to the Singleton family that brought him back to that place.

On June 24, 1863, Union troops moved through Hoovers Gap and the sound of the guns reached Fairfield, only five miles away. Soon the Confederates were gone from the area, and George was once more a free man. At the nearby town of Wartrace, a recruiting office was opened, seeking African-American troops for the United States. George enlisted, and when asked for his last name, replied, "Singleton." It was not uncommon for those who had been slaves to have no last name.

George was a good soldier. He accompanied his regiment all over Middle Tennessee, guarding railroads, skirmishing with rebel raiders and guerrillas, and taking part in the battle of Nashville in December 1864. With the exception of the battle of Nashville, George did not participate in events that made history or changed the course of the war. But his life was still in danger, and as any soldier knows, faithful service is more difficult in surroundings that are routine, even dull. And George was loyal to his soldier's oath. Because of his skill as a soldier and his sense of responsibility, he was promoted to corporal, then to sergeant, the highest rank then open to African Americans in the U.S. Army. His army service record shows that George was, indeed, a valiant sergeant.

In the spring of 1866, when he was discharged from the Army, George needed work. His one skill was that of farmer, and there was one farm he knew better than any other. He turned his steps back toward Fairfield.

At Fairfield, Robert also needed a way to earn a living. He had survived two and one-half years in a prison camp in which almost 20 percent of the inmates died, a death rate as high as the notorious prison camp near Andersonville, Georgia. Robert still had the family farm and a little livestock, but a one-legged man could not plow with a team of mules. Then George showed up.

The ex-Confederate captain and the ex-Union sergeant, former master and former slave, made a deal. George would be foreman of any workers he could recruit to farm the place, while Robert managed the financial affairs. This arrangement lasted for the remainder of both their lives.

Today, in the cemetery at Mt. Zion Baptist Church in Fairfield, Tennessee, there are two graves almost side by side. One stone is marked:

ROBERT SINGLETON

CAPTAIN 17TH TENN INF

C.S.A.

The other reads:

GEORGE SINGLETON

SERGEANT 15TH U.S.C.T.

U.S.A.

Every May, in a solemn but joyful ceremony, the Singletons, white and black, place flowers on the graves of their ancestors and visit a while to renew old acquaintances. A favorite story always told is that of the loyal servant–valiant sergeant.

Author's note: The letters Robert Singleton wrote his mother, including those from Fort Delaware, can be read on the Internet at www .cwrc.org/c_war/singleton.html. At the same site are a picture of Sergeant George Singleton in uniform and a copy of his service record.

THUNDER AND LIGHTNING
AT HOOVERS GAP

1863

The rain poured in torrents while lightning flashed across the sky, and thunder rolled and echoed from the hills. Amidst this storm a different kind of thunder and lightning poured from the muzzles of the Spencer repeating rifles in the hands of the men of Colonel John Wilder's brigade of mounted infantry. On June 24, 1863, at Hoovers Gap, Tennessee, a new chapter was begun in the chronicles of warfare. For the first time in military history, a battle was being fought using repeating rifles.

The road to Hoovers Gap had not been an easy one for Colonel Wilder and his men. For most of them it had begun about a year earlier when they had enlisted in Indiana and Illinois. As they rode into Hoovers Gap, the brigade consisted of the 17th Indiana, the 72nd Indiana, the 123rd Illinois, and the 98th Illinois, all mounted infantry regiments. Artillery support was provided by the Eighteenth Indiana Artillery, a battery commanded by Eli Lilly. After the war Lilly would found an internationally famous pharmaceutical company.

Colonel Wilder was not a West Pointer, nor did he have any other military experience prior to the outbreak of the rebellion. His military success stemmed from his burning desire to be a winner and from his successful background as an engineer and a business-man. Wilder had indeed made a success in business in Greensburg, Indiana, where he opened a machine shop in which he manufactured hydraulic machinery of his own design.

Perhaps it was these mechanical skills that caused Wilder to pay attention when Christopher Spencer showed up in the bivouacs of the Army of the Cumberland to demonstrate his new repeating rifle. The Spencer rifle was a .52-caliber weapon weighing ten pounds. In the stock was a tube magazine that held seven rimfire cartridges. Additional magazines could be loaded in advance and carried into battle. Swinging the trigger guard down and forward ejected the spent cartridge and fed a fresh round into the firing chamber. The rifle was cocked by pulling back the hammer with the thumb. It had a rear leaf sight that registered two thousand yards, and the rifle was dead accurate up to three hundred yards.

Having seen a demonstration of the rifle, the men of Wilder's brigade knew they wanted the weapon, but there was a problem. The government would not furnish them with the Spencers. But Wilder would not be stopped by bureaucratic regulations where the efficiency and welfare of his men were concerned. Receiving a furlough, Wilder returned to his hometown and negotiated a loan with his bank to cover the cost of a repeater for each man in his command. The men then signed a promissory note to pay for their individual rifles at a fixed amount per payday. Because the rifles cost $35 and a private received $16 a month, the soldiers were investing heavily in their own armament. As spring advanced and as supplies gradually accumulated, Wilder made ready to move. The village of Manchester was the primary target for all the army, and Wilder's men would lead the way. At three o'clock on the morning of June 24, 1863, in a steady rain, Wilder's men broke camp and moved toward the Manchester Pike.

The Manchester Pike wound for four miles through Hoovers Gap, which had hills two hundred to three hundred feet high on each side and was so narrow in places that two wagons could not pass each other. Wilder's brigade splashed along an increasingly muddy road, waiting for the Confederates to offer resistance. Major John Connolley described the event:

> *Soon after daylight a heavy rain commenced falling which continued without interruption all day and night, and has continued ever since, with only a few hours cessation at a time. About noon [June 24] the first gun was fired, and then we pushed ahead rapidly, for we were nearing the formidable "Hoovers Gap," which it was supposed would cost a great many lives to pass through and our brigade commander determined to surprise the enemy if possible, by a rapid march, and make a bold dash to pass through the "Gap" and hold it with our brigade alone until the rest of the army could get up. We soon came into the camp of a regiment of cavalry which was so much surprised by our sudden appearance that they scattered through the woods and over the hills in every direction, but we didn't stop for anything, on we pushed, our boys, with their Spencer rifles, keeping up a continual popping in front. Soon we reached the celebrated Gap on the run.*

As a Confederate brigade under William Bate drove in Wilder's skirmishers, Wilder shifted men to reinforce his right, nearest the advancing enemy. Bate pressed his attack on Wilder's right. Although the ground was favorable for defense, Wilder had to send three more regiments to his right to counter the Confederate attack. Seeing so much weight going to his enemy's right, Bate made a lunge for Lilly's six artillery pieces. The Twentieth Tennessee came around the shoulder of a hill and started across a relatively level piece of ground toward the battery. Sweeping forward despite rifle fire from the flanks and the fire of Lilly's guns in front, the Tennesseans came within twenty yards of Lilly's guns when the 123rd Illinois rose up from a depression where they had been lying and erupted like a volcano in the Southerners' faces. Despite the pouring rain, every man in the 123rd got off seven shots and did so in less than a minute. No troops could withstand a volley of that intensity. About 150 rebel casualties littered the ground in front of Lilly's position.

About this time Captain Thomas Rice, adjutant to General John Fulton Reynolds, arrived with orders for Wilder to withdraw, because Reynolds considered him to be too far advanced and in an exposed position. Wilder refused the order, saying he could hold his position and that he would assume the responsibility for his actions. Later, Major General George Thomas, Wilder's corps commander, would congratulate him, saying, "You saved the lives of a thousand men by your gallant conduct today. I didn't expect to get the Gap for three days."

All that day the story was much the same. Any Confederate advance was immediately met by a volcano of fire coming from the muzzles of Spencer repeating rifles in the hands of Wilder's men. Wilder knew he was doing something unique in the history of warfare. He noted in his after-action report: "The effect of our terrible fire was overwhelming to our opponents, who bravely tried to withstand its effects. No human being could successfully face such an avalanche of destruction as our continuous fire swept through their lines."

June 24 ended in rain and fog at Hoovers Gap. But the sun set that day not just on yet another bloody field where a few hundred men from North and South had engaged each other in combat; the sun also set on an era, the era of muzzle-loading weapons. From Hoovers Gap forward, combat belonged to the repeater. The old technology would hang on for a little longer, but its heyday was done. The engagement at Hoovers Gap was a turning point in the history of warfare.

THE OLD MAN OF GETTYSBURG

1863

Civil War armies were notorious for containing eccentric individuals, both officers and enlisted men, and battles often brought their eccentricities into sharp display. But of all the eccentric characters of that war, none would loom larger than the "Old Man" who took part in the largest battle of the war, John Burns of Gettysburg.

Ever since the Confederate victory at Chancellorsville, Virginia, in May 1863, it had been obvious that Robert E. Lee would try to bring his Army of Northern Virginia across the Mason-Dixon Line. With two Union armies pushing deep into the South, one at Vicksburg, Mississippi, and one in Middle Tennessee, anyone could predict that Lee would move north in an attempt to divert Union resources and relieve the pressure on the Confederacy.

The possibility of a rebel invasion caused quite a stir among the people of the North. They had no experience with war, unlike the civilians of the South. But the Northerners had read newspaper accounts of what their armies had done in the South; they had, perhaps, talked to local boys who had come home from the army telling tales of both incidental and deliberate devastation inflicted on the South. And now the war was coming their way!

Of course many people blustered and boasted of what they would do if the rebels came to their neighborhood or bothered their property. And of course most knew such was only talk. But in Gettysburg, Pennsylvania, John Burns listened to his neighbors and said not much at all. That did not surprise many of them for John was considered not to be especially intelligent and something of a town "character." John was a cobbler by trade and a veteran of the War of 1812. When the Civil War began, he had volunteered for the Pennsylvania reserves but had been laughed at and told to go home where a man his age belonged. Determined to do his part, he served for a time as a wagoner, but the work and exposure to the elements were too much for him, so he went back to his cobbler shop in Gettysburg. There he would remain until, one day, the war came to him.

From late June onward Confederate troops came swinging up into Pennsylvania. In June a brigade of them paid a visit to Gettysburg, looking for shoes. Perhaps some of the "Rebs" came into John Burns's shop, looking for footwear. Because these soldiers had been ordered to pay for everything they took and not to steal anything, they may have left him with a pocketful of Confederate banknotes—and no shoes on his shelves. At any rate, when gunfire erupted on a ridge west of Gettysburg early on the morning of July 1, 1863, John was ready to defend his town.

Old John Burns put on his best Sunday clothes to go to war. Given the dust and dirt of that July day, that seems strange. His wife certainly didn't like it. It was her job to keep the old man neat and clean, and this looked to be the beginning of a major scrubbing job. It was not hard for John to find a rifle and cartridge box. Wounded soldiers were beginning to come trickling into town as the fight grew in intensity. Slogging along the road, he fell in with one of the most noted units in all the Union Army of the Potomac, the Iron Brigade, part of a division commanded by Major General James Wadsworth. These men were about to get into the worst fight of their entire career, a career that had included much desperate fighting, and John Burns would be in this fight with them.

Wadsworth's division came on the field just in time to stop a successful Confederate attack and to roll back the rebels. Soon, however, more gray-clad troops came on the field, and it was the Yankees' turn to give ground. Pushed back to the campus of the Lutheran Seminary on the outskirts of town, the blue line dug in its heels for a final stand.

In all the advance and retreat, John had done his part. He had somehow kept up with the young men in the Iron Brigade and had even won their respect for his coolness under fire. Some of the soldiers were even crediting John with shooting a Confederate officer off his horse. Now, however, the ranks were thin, throats were parched, ammunition was low, and artillery pounded the Union line. Covered with dust, a couple of bullet holes in his coat, John Burns still held his place. Suddenly, there was the unmistakable sound of a rifle slug hitting a body. John doubled over and fell to his knees. After a few minutes he stood up unsteadily, gasping for breath. The bullet had struck his belt buckle!

Ordered to the rear, John started for town but was hit twice more, one a slight flesh wound and the other a disabling blow to his ankle. Just as he got to town, the Union line on Seminary Ridge collapsed and Confederates flooded into Gettysburg. Soon John found himself a prisoner.

After his wounds had been dressed by a rebel doctor, John was told to go home. Tradition says he hailed another civilian and sent him with a message to his wife, "Tell the old woman to fetch the wagon. I can't walk." His wife sent back the reply, "The old fool! He is too old to be fighting. He's probably ruined his good clothes and won't be able to work for weeks. The rebels can have him!"

John Burns was more respected by others than by his wife. When President Abraham Lincoln came to town to make a speech dedicating the soldiers' graves in the cemetery, he asked to meet John. John became known as "The Hero of Gettysburg" and was awarded a pension as a Union soldier. John Burns died in 1872 and is buried on Cemetery Hill, where the Union army won its victory on July 2 and 3, 1863. His grave is topped by a statue of his likeness, rifle firmly in hand, facing the Confederate lines.

The Old Man of Gettysburg still stands ready to defend his town.

EVEN HIS ENEMY
CONGRATULATED HIM

1863

Frank Baldwin was a modest man, but he was determined, and he would prove to the world that he was brave. He was so brave that even his enemies would congratulate him.

In September 1863 the Union army was facing a crisis. After successfully maneuvering the Confederate army under General Braxton Bragg out of Tennessee in July, Union General William Rosecrans had found himself defeated at the battle of Chickamauga in northern Georgia. Now, as the summer turned to fall, Rosecrans and his Army of the Cumberland were trapped in Chattanooga, Tennessee. Union forces were gathering to rescue them, but the success of the attempt depended on the Union forces keeping control of the railroads, especially the Nashville and Chattanooga Railroad that ran through Murfreesboro.

At Murfreesboro, Union troops had used hundreds of African-American laborers to build the largest earthwork fort ever constructed in North America, Fort Rosecrans. But even this massive fortification, with its huge cannons, could protect only a limited area. To ensure that the railroad stayed safe from Confederate raiders, small wooden stockades had to be built at every bridge the railroad crossed. In addition, blockhouses of large logs were constructed at every culvert.

And the Confederates were coming! General Joseph Wheeler and several thousand rebel cavalrymen were riding hell for leather all across Middle Tennessee. They knew that if they could wreck the railroad thoroughly, the Union rescue attempt would be slowed so much that the Yankees in Chattanooga might be starved into surrender.

First Lieutenant Frank Baldwin was in command of Company D, Nineteenth Michigan. He was a veteran soldier, having first enlisted in 1861 when he was nineteen years old. Baldwin had been born in Manchester, Michigan, and attended the public school in the town of Constantine before enrolling in Hillsdale College. Dark complexioned, stocky, and of average height, Baldwin liked the army. Indeed he would go on to make a career in the military, staying in the cavalry when the Civil War was over, seeing action against the Indians in Texas and fighting guerrillas in the Philippines during the Spanish-American War. Now, at twenty-one, he found himself and fifty men manning a stockade overlooking a 200-foot-long trestle on the railroad four miles outside Murfreesboro. The stockade was constructed of squared timbers sunk two feet into the ground and standing eight feet in the air. Loopholes at a convenient height allowed the defenders to fire at attackers while remaining under cover. All trees and brush had been cleared from a wide area around the stockade, so there was a good field of fire, but Baldwin wasn't satisfied. In his pocket he had written orders instructing him to hold the post until relieved. Holding the stockade would be easy enough if only riflemen came against it, but if the rebels showed up with artillery, Baldwin knew his stockade walls would provide about as much protection as toothpicks. As the best precaution he could take, Baldwin had his men shovel dirt against the bottom of the stockade wall, creating a berm about two feet high.

On the morning of October 4, 1863, several parties of Confederate cavalry were in view, nosing closer and closer to the stockade. Baldwin sent off several runners to bring help from Murfreesboro, but no reinforcements appeared. Probably all the runners were captured or shot by the Confederates. Baldwin had enough experience in combat to know that he was seeing the scouts and advance parties of the Confederates. As soon as they were sure he was isolated, the main body would come up. Sure enough, the next morning, just as dawn was breaking through a light mist, a Confederate officer came riding toward the stockade, waving a flag of truce.

"Lieutenant, I am instructed to say, on behalf of General Joseph Wheeler, that you are surrounded and cut off. The general demands your immediate surrender."

"Captain, please inform your general that I have strict orders to prevent him from destroying this trestle, and that is just what I intend to do as long as I'm able."

"Lieutenant, those are brave and honorable words, but you don't have a chance. We have artillery, so on your head be it."

Soon a thin line of gray-clad dismounted cavalry began pressing toward the stockade. Baldwin's men stood to their loopholes and opened fire. Quickly, the gray cavalry dropped to the ground and returned the fire, only to have their bullets thud harmlessly into the timbers of the stockade. Then atop a low ridge some six hundred yards away appeared a battery of cannon.

With the first puff of smoke, a shell came screaming over the stockade. The second hit the wall, cutting off the timber and sending jagged splinters of wood flying like spears across the interior of the small enclosure. Every shot hit the wall, and the cannon were too far away for the Michiganders' rifles to be effective against them. In a few minutes it was all over. The stockade was blown to smithereens. Of Baldwin's fifty men, forty-nine were dead or wounded. Regretfully, Frank Baldwin waved a towel as a flag of surrender.

Out of the smoke came riding a small, dapper man in a neat, gray uniform. Three stars surrounded by a wreath on his collar indicated his rank as a general.

"Lieutenant, this is the biggest piece of foolishness I have ever seen. I have not lost a man, and your command has been wiped out. It is mere luck you aren't a casualty yourself. If you had surrendered, you would have saved a lot of good men from death and suffering."

Saluting, Baldwin replied, "General, please read this paper. It is from my commanding officer and it orders me to hold this position until relieved. As yet, I have not been relieved."

General Wheeler looked at the order. "Lieutenant, under the terms of these orders, you have done what is right. I will not take any of your command as prisoners of war. I will destroy this trestle, and then you and the surviving members of your command can remain here to bury your dead. Your friends will come out from Murfreesboro as soon as I am gone. I congratulate you on your devotion to duty."

And so it was. Frank Baldwin's commanding officer was so impressed by the bravery and determination shown in the defense of the trestle that Baldwin was nominated for the Medal of Honor. For some reason, however, the nomination did not result in the medal's being given. However, on July 20, 1864, near Atlanta, Georgia, and again on November 8, 1874, at McClellan's Creek in Texas, Frank Baldwin twice more proved his bravery and devotion and became the second person in the history of the United States to win the Medal of Honor twice. He is still the only person to have been nominated for the award a third time.

A CONFEDERATE NAVAL CAPTAIN
FREES A SLAVE

1863

"Sail ho!" That was the third time in two days the cry had gone up from the masthead of the CSS *Alabama*. Her captain, Raphael Semmes, had made a wise decision in taking his ship to the sea lanes off the coast of Newfoundland. There were rich pickings to be made of northern ships headed for British and European ports. Although the chase began at noon, it was almost 4:00 p.m. before the *Alabama* was close enough to fire a warning shot across the bow of the 1,300-ton merchant ship *Tonawanda*. As soon as the cannon fired, the merchantman came into the wind and a small boat carrying an officer and men from the *Alabama* rowed across to take possession. Not long afterward, the officers, crew, and passengers from the *Tonawanda* were aboard the *Alabama*.

As Captain Semmes talked with the commander of his most recent capture, a smile crossed his face. Semmes had just been informed that one of the passengers on the *Tonawanda* was a wealthy man from Delaware who was accompanied by his slave, a 17-year-old named David H. White.

Although often overlooked today, the fact is that five slave states remained in the Union. Missouri, Kentucky, Maryland, Delaware, and New Jersey all retained the institution of slavery as legal. After all, slavery was protected by the U. S. Constitution and would remain protected until 1865 when the Thirteenth Amendment to the Constitution was adopted. Although Abraham Lincoln had proposed the Emancipation Proclamation in September 1862, the terms of the Proclamation exempted northern slaves, leaving them in bondage. It was, however, the policy of the U.S. military to treat southern slaves as "contraband of war," property valuable to the Confederate war effort, and to remove the slaves from the custody of the slave owner in order to weaken the Confederacy. Semmes smiled because his ironic sense of humor recognized that now he could do the same thing in reverse. He could emancipate the slave of a northern slave owner. David White and his owner were called into Semmes's cabin, and in the presence of witnesses, a document was drawn up stating that White was no longer the property of the slave owner from Delaware. White was now free to choose his own course.

The *Alabama* was crowded with the prisoners taken from three ships captured earlier, so all the captives were placed, under guard, on the *Tonawanda*. Two days later, yet another ship fell victim to the *Alabama,* and the crew of this ship was also placed aboard *Tonawanda*. The captain of the *Tonawanda* was then told that if he posted a bond with Semmes, he would be allowed to take his ship, loaded with the captured sailors, and set sail for New York City. Before releasing the men, Semmes, as he always did, asked if anyone wanted to join the crew of the *Alabama*. Among the handful of volunteers was David White. The addition of White to the crew was unusual in that he was a former slave, but the *Alabama* carried a very mixed crew. The officers were all from the Southern states, but the crew members came from numerous European nations and included some West Indians and Asians. The pay aboard the *Alabama* was higher than on merchant ships, and money was the motivation for many crew members, although some were simply adventurers who liked the life aboard a commerce raider.

As an unskilled landsman, David was assigned to duty as a wardroom steward, waiting on the table for the ship's officers. Of all the men he served in the wardroom, David liked most Dr. Francis Galt, the ship's surgeon. Perhaps this relationship developed because in combat the stewards often worked as stretcher bearers, assisting the doctor.

The *Alabama,* with David White as a crewman, sailed up and down the northeastern coast of the United States and Canada, capturing ships registered in the United States. Then Semmes took his command across the Atlantic to play havoc with the merchant trade along the coast of Europe. Crossing westward at the end of 1862, the Confederate raider disrupted shipping in the Caribbean before entering the Gulf of Mexico. Off the Texas port of Galveston, the *Alabama* engaged in combat with the USS *Hatteras* and sank the Union warship. David White became a veteran of naval combat.

In November the *Alabama* sailed into Fort-de-France on the island of Martinique to replenish provisions and to allow the crew shore leave. When time came to leave harbor, Semmes found about twenty of his crew hungover, half-drunk on rum they had brought aboard, and unwilling to obey orders. The officers of the ship armed themselves with pistols and subdued the mutineers. Under the Articles of War, Semmes could have hanged the men, but he took a different approach. The men, in handcuffs and leg irons, were piled on the deck. David White, and others, manned a fire pump that pulled up seawater from over the side, and they doused the mutineers with water. At first the mutineers laughed, but they soon became chilled through. The "shower bath" continued for almost two hours until the men were soaked, sober, and ready to obey orders. Following this incident, it was a standing joke on the *Alabama* that the wardroom steward, David White, knew how to water the rum!

New adventures were still to come for White and the *Alabama*. Leaving the Gulf, the ship steered into the South Atlantic and cruised off the coast of Brazil, capturing another dozen U.S. merchant ships. Then Semmes turned the bow of his ship east, all the way to Africa. Rounding the Cape of Good Hope, the *Alabama* carried the war into Asian waters. For all of 1863 and into the spring of 1864, David White saw lands and peoples he had never even dreamed of until he was emancipated by a Confederate sailor.

In March 1864, the *Alabama* anchored at Cape Town, South Africa. In Dixie the war was reaching a crisis, so Semmes again led his crew on a western crossing of the Atlantic and then eastward back to Europe, capturing and sinking U.S. merchant ships as he went.

By now the *Alabama,* and David White, had been at sea twenty months and had sailed 75,000 miles. Two hundred and ninety-four U.S.-registered ships had been captured. But the crew needed rest and the ship required repairs. On June 10, 1864, the CSS *Alabama* entered the port of Cherbourg. David White had one more adventure awaiting him, although he did not know it.

On June 14, the USS *Kearsarge* anchored outside the port of Cherbourg. Under the law governing foreign warships in a neutral port, the *Alabama* had only a limited time before she had to leave. The *Kearsarge* was waiting. On the morning of June 19, Semmes called his crew to attention. All those not assigned stations on one of the guns or required to make up the engine room crew had been allowed to leave the ship earlier. But, as the crew fell in for sailing,

David White was among them. Although a wardroom steward, White had volunteered for combat.

At 11:00 a.m. the battle between the *Alabama* and the *Kearsarge* was joined. Just over an hour later, the Confederate raider slipped beneath the waves. Among those who went down with the ship was David White. He gave his life for emancipation.

A DARING PRISON ESCAPE

1863

He felt as if the walls of his tiny cell were closing in on him—not that they would have far to move. The cell was only forty-two inches by eighty-four inches, barely room for a cot, and he had to spend twelve hours a day in the cramped quarters. He was not meant for such a life. He was a cavalry man; indeed, he was a bold and dashing raider, John Hunt Morgan of Lexington, Kentucky. He was meant for life on horseback in the open air, not for this stinking little hole in the Ohio State Penitentiary. And it was for the open air he was bound.

John Hunt Morgan had become a name to reckon with in northern circles. A bold and efficient cavalry raider, he had risen in rank from captain to brigadier general in only nine months. No railroad conductor felt confident of his train reaching its destination if Morgan was on a raid. But in the summer of 1863, Morgan had overreached himself. Granted permission by his commanding general, Braxton Bragg, to raid into his home state of Kentucky to disrupt Union supplies, Morgan took it upon himself to cross the Ohio River on July 13, 1863.

Although he created consternation among the farmers in southern Ohio, Morgan also had stirred up a hornet's nest. The local militia, many of them Union army veterans, barricaded every town and blocked every road. On July 26, 1863, exhausted by thirteen days in the saddle for up to twenty-one hours a day, Morgan surrendered with what was left of his force. But instead of being treated as prisoners of war, Morgan and the officers of his command were taken to the Ohio State Penitentiary in Columbus, where they were stripped, scrubbed with stiff brushes, and clean shaven—an insult to men in a time when whiskers were considered a sign of manhood.

As soon as they could, Morgan and his officers began planning an escape. One of Morgan's men, Thomas H. Hines, observed that no dampness accumulated on the floor of his cell and guessed that there must be an airshaft beneath his floor. Soon a plan was hatched. Knives were stolen from the prison mess hall to use for digging. Hines offered to sweep out his own cell, and the prison janitor readily accepted this proposal. Now he was free to dig. On November 4, 1863, the first scrapes were made in the concrete floor of the cell.

At first digging went on so slowly that disposing of the debris was no problem, but as the plotters began to make some headway with their excavation, a hiding place for the pieces of broken concrete had to be found. The only solution they could think of was to stuff the material into a mattress. Soon Hines found himself sleeping on a sack of broken bricks and chunks of concrete.

They dug down steadily, through six inches of cement, a five-inch bed of lime mortar, and three layers of brick. On the fourth day of digging, they broke through to the airshaft, six feet wide and four feet tall. Then they found they would have to dig through the five-foot-thick foundation of the building, tunnel twelve feet to the wall around the prison, and dig four feet to the surface of the ground. Then they would have to scale the wall with a rope braided from strips of bed ticking and drop down the far side of the wall. To make matters even more complicated, the airshaft had only one entrance, and that was in Hines's cell. To allow others a chance to escape, the concrete in their cell floors would be scraped away from below until only a thin layer was left. Progress seemed slow, but in less than two weeks all was ready.

November 27, 1863, dawned cold and gloomy. All day fitful rain showers fell. Darkness came early in the afternoon, and at seven o'clock, each prisoner was ordered by prison guards to his unlighted cell for the next twelve hours. Morgan quietly went into his brother Dick's cell while Dick went to the second-floor cell of John. Because escape from the second floor was impossible, Dick Morgan was giving up his chance so his more famous and higher-ranking brother could break out of prison. It was thought that John Morgan would be of more service to the Confederacy, and that his escape would call attention to the plight of the other men.

That was when it stared to feel as if the walls were closing in. The men planning to escape had to wait until midnight, when the last bed check was made. Never had time passed so slowly. At last the footsteps of the guard echoed down the corridor, and the light of his lantern played over the sleeping forms.

Morgan had been lying with his back to the door so that he would not be discovered in the wrong cell. Now he got up, and after hastily stuffing some straw into his uniform coat so it would appear someone was still in the bed, he stomped on the thin layer of concrete covering the hole in the floor.

Waiting for Morgan in the airshaft were five other men. As quickly as rats, they scurried along the shaft, entered their tunnel, and crawled to the end. Carefully, the first man probed the dirt until it collapsed on them, opening a way to the surface. Now they were in the open air, but they were still inside the walls of the prison.

Quietly, they flung their homemade rope upward and felt satisfaction as the grapple hook made from a stolen stove poker caught. Silently, one after the other, they scaled the wall. Shifting the rope, they slid down the outside of the prison wall. To their horror, only sixty yards away blazed a bonfire with several prison guards clustered around it. As quickly as silence would allow, the men slipped into the darkness, heading in separate directions. Morgan and Hines had decided to stay together and made for the train station. Because suspicion would be focused on travelers going north toward Canada, the usual route followed by escaping Confederates, Morgan and Hines decided to make for Cincinnati. Few people would expect Confederate escapees to make directly for the South. Hiding in plain sight would probably be the most effective plan of concealment. Using money that had been smuggled to them by a Confederate sympathizer, they bought tickets for Cincinnati.

Boarding the train, Morgan decided boldness was the best policy and took a seat beside a Union officer. A lively conversation soon led to the offer of a drink from the officer's brandy flask. As the train passed the walls of the penitentiary, the Union officer said, "That's where they've got old John Morgan."

"Yes," replied Morgan, "and I hope they always guard him as well as they do now!"

There were close calls and hair-raising adventures ahead, but John Morgan made it safely back to Confederate territory, only to lose his life during a Union surprise attack on his command at Greenville, Tennessee, on September 4, 1864.

GUNPOWDER FROM URINE

1863–65

The rebel soldier fumbled in his cartridge box and drew out another round of ammunition. He raised the paper cylinder to his mouth and prepared to bite off the end so he could pour the contents down the barrel of his rifle. Then, just before biting into the paper, he remembered how the Confederacy made gunpowder, and he gagged slightly. But, as General Sherman would one day say, "War is hell," so he put the paper between his teeth and ripped the cartridge open, getting a few grains of black powder on his tongue and lips.

Civil War–era gunpowder was made from a recipe calling for a mixture of 75 percent potassium nitrate or "niter," 15 percent charcoal, and 10 percent sulfur. Getting charcoal was not a problem because the South possessed extensive woodlands. Sulfur was obtained by roasting iron pyrite, or fool's gold. But obtaining niter posed a problem. A great deal of the niter, also called saltpeter, used in the prewar South came from abroad. In the North, with open ports, the flow of niter from South America continued unabated, but in the blockaded South, supplies began to run short despite a small supply brought in by blockade runners. To solve the problem the South turned to Josiah Gorgas, a native of Pennsylvania.

Gorgas was a West Point graduate with considerable experience in the Ordnance Bureau of the United States Army. While stationed at Mount Vernon Arsenal near Mobile, Alabama, he had fallen in love with and married Amelia Gayle, daughter of a former governor of the state. When the Civil War began, Gorgas joined the Confederate forces and was soon placed in charge of ordnance for the new nation.

It is not a stereotype to say that the Confederacy was weak in industrial capacity. About 20 percent of the industrial capacity listed in the 1860 census was located in the states that formed the Confederacy. These same states produced just over nine hundred tons of iron in 1860, mostly in small, scattered furnaces. This meant the materials of war could be secured only by the exercise of ingenuity, and then only with difficulty. For example, the Confederacy had an excellent source of copper in the mines located at Copper Hill, Tennessee. Copper was essential to the war effort because in order to fire his rifle, a soldier had to place a percussion cap made of copper and containing an explosive charge on a nipple on the barrel of his weapon. This cap was struck by the hammer of the gun, and a flash of fire shot through a hole beneath the nipple into the chamber of the rifle, igniting the charge. Gorgas could get his hands on plenty of copper, but the flash of fire from the copper cap was caused by fulminate of mercury, and the mercury came from Mexico. Since communications with Mexico were cut off following the fall of Vicksburg to Union troops on July 4, 1863, a substitute had to be found for mercury. Gorgas and an associate, John Mallett, found that chlorate of potash or a mixture of sulfur and antimony could be used to make percussion caps.

Gunpowder remained the great challenge. Since imports were cut off, where could the Confederacy get niter? Josiah Gorgas knew that caves where bats had roosted for centuries would be a rich source of niter. The bat guano (droppings) was scraped up and placed in large vats. Water was allowed to seep slowly through the vats and collect in pans. When the water that had seeped through was boiled away, niter crystals were left behind. Soon every cave in the South was being scoured for guano, with a result being that today almost every county in the southern mountains has a "saltpeter cave." Men working in the caves digging guano, leaching and boiling niter water, and then grinding the crystals were so valuable to the war effort that Gorgas convinced the Confederate government to exempt them from the draft. The Union, however, treated such men as prisoners of war, not as civilians, if captured.

Of course the supply of guano from these caves was not limitless, and some locations were lost as the Union armies advanced, so another source of niter had to be found. At first Gorgas turned to dirt collected from smokehouses and barns, but this still was not enough. Then Gorgas discovered an inexhaustible, constantly renewed source for niter. With the assistance of Isaac M. St. John, Gorgas began the construction of niter beds.

Near each city, town, and village in Confederate territory, long wooden frames many feet long and with sides several inches in height were built. The earth in the bottom of the frames was scraped down to the bare mineral soil, and the frames were then filled with a mixture of limestone, wood ashes, and old mortar (mortar of that period contained a large amount of lime) to form a base. This mixture was then kept wet with urine. After several months of soaking with urine, the base of the niter bed would be leached with water and the resultant liquid boiled down. The result was pure niter crystals.

In order to collect enough urine, patriotic appeals were made to save chamber lye for use by the niter works. Because this was before the days of indoor plumbing, every household had several chamber pots, and the collection of the urine was somewhat easier than would be the case today. Even in the Victorian age, this method of making niter was an irresistible target for satire, and soon a ribald poem was making the rounds, poking fun at John Haralson, the niter agent for Selma, Alabama. It began:

> *John Haralson, John Haralson, you are a*
> *funny creature.*
> *You have given to this war, a new and*
> *curious feature.*

The poem quickly degenerated from that point on.

Not satisfied with this accomplishment, at Augusta, Georgia, Gorgas constructed the Augusta Ordnance Bureau, a unique factory where gunpowder was produced in assembly line fashion. Shortages forced Gorgas to make several changes in the traditional methods of producing gunpowder, and almost every change proved to be an improvement in the process. The gunpowder produced from urine was hailed by neutral observers as "the finest in the world." Bizarre though it seems, the scheme developed by Josiah Gorgas and his assistants produced about 4 million pounds of niter and kept the guns of the Confederacy blazing through four years of warfare.

Author's note: In 1898 William C. Gorgas, the son of Josiah Gorgas, served in the United States Army as a doctor during the Spanish-American War. Experiments he began while stationed in Cuba led to the discovery of the cause and cure of both malaria and yellow fever. The control of these diseases, in turn, made possible the construction of the Panama Canal.

THE HISTORIC VOYAGE
OF THE CSS *HUNLEY*

1864

As the American Civil War dragged on, it became obvious to H. L. Hunley that the Union naval blockade was choking the South to death. But he had an idea about how that could be changed. If the Confederacy could not control the surface of the water, perhaps they could fight from below the water. Eventually, that idea would cost Hunley his life.

Horace Lawson Hunley, a native of Tennessee, was living in New Orleans at the outbreak of the war. With two partners, Hunley financed the construction of a submarine, *Pioneer*, built to operate as a private warship. If an enemy ship were sunk, the partners would collect a bounty. The vessel would submerge by opening a valve to allow water to enter a ballast tank. To surface, a hand pump would force the water out. Mobility was provided by men turning cranks connected to a drive shaft for a propeller. This experimental vessel was scuttled when New Orleans was captured by Union forces.

Moving to Mobile, Alabama, Hunley and his friends built another submarine, *American Diver,* only to see it sink in Mobile Bay with all hands aboard. Not discouraged, Hunley and his partners worked to produce yet a third boat, which was named in Hunley's honor. Like so much built by the Confederates, this boat was make-shift. Most of its body was made from a boiler for a locomotive, with conical extensions attached to both ends to make it more stream-lined. The *Hunley* was, however, a true submersible craft, capable of operating underwater. At the request of General Pierre Beauregard, the *Hunley* was shipped by railroad to Charleston, South Carolina, to attempt to raise the blockade there. Lieutenant John A. Payne was placed in command of the boat, which was taken over by the Con-federate navy despite its having been privately built.

Payne and a volunteer crew ventured out to attack a Union ship in Charleston Harbor, but disaster struck when Payne stepped on a lever controlling the dive planes, causing the boat to plunge below the surface while the hatch was still open. Four of the nine men aboard escaped, but the others drowned. Following salvage opera-tions, Payne tried again, only to have *Hunley* swamped by the wake of a passing boat, this time with the loss of six crew members. The ship was again raised from the bottom of the harbor, and H. L. Hun-ley took charge of the boat with a crew brought from Mobile. On October 15, 1863, *Hunley* failed to resurface from a practice dive. For the third time, *Hunley* had proved to be an iron coffin for her crew—and this time for its inventor.

A new crew was ready to go aboard *Hunley* even before she was raised again. The new commander was Lieutenant George E. Dixon, another of the partners in the venture to build the boat. Dixon and his men knew their lives were on the line every time they went aboard *Hunley,* so they practiced their roles carefully and looked hard for modifications that would make their vessel more safe and seaworthy. On February 17, 1864, the men felt they were ready to take the *Hunley* to war once again.

About three miles off Breach Inlet, one of the entrances to Charleston Harbor, the USS *Housatonic* lay at anchor. The sailors in the blockading fleet knew the Confederates were experimenting with underwater vessels, and the admiral in command of the fleet, Rear Admiral John A. Dahlgren, had ordered his ships to anchor in shallow water so there would be less chance of a Confederate submarine going under them. Even so, CSS *Hunley* was on her way.

For two hours the crew cranked away, propelling *Hunley* across the choppy surface of the harbor. The sub was designed to have only limited buoyancy, and the only thing above the water was a combing around the hatch. From there Lieutenant Dixon kept watch. Projecting several feet in front of the bow was a slender iron rod, at the end of which was fixed a cylinder containing ninety pounds of gunpowder. A harpoon-like blade was fixed to penetrate the side of the target and hold the explosive in place until it was detonated by a lanyard.

Inside the cramped hull of the *Hunley,* tension was high. Clear in the minds of all aboard was the fate of each of the first three crews, but also clear was their chance to make history and strike a blow for their country.

At 8:45 p.m. Acting Master J. K. Crosby, officer of the deck aboard *Housatonic,* spotted what appeared to be a log floating about one hundred yards away but moving toward his ship. Immediately, Crosby ordered the anchor chair slipped, the engine reversed, and all hands called to battle stations. The call came too late. A jar was felt forward of the mizzenmast on the starboard side as the harpoon slammed into the side of *Housatonic*. About one minute later there was a huge explosion as the torpedo was detonated. With a hole several square feet in her hull, the ship plunged quickly to the bottom of the harbor. Fortunately, the water was shallow enough in that area that the masts and rigging stayed above the surface. All except five members of the crew survived by climbing into the rigging.

Hunley had just made history. For the first time in the annals of warfare, a submarine had destroyed a surface ship. Backing away into the darkness, followed by a hail of small arms fire, the boat turned slowly toward Charleston and home. Apparently, Lieutenant Dixon steered toward the main harbor entrance, where the incoming tide would help push the boat toward her berth. Forty-five minutes after sinking *Housatonic*, *Hunley* signaled one of the shore defenses, Battery Marshal, that she was on her way home. She never arrived.

In 1995 the underwater grave of the *Hunley* and her fourth crew was discovered, though E. Lee Spence of Charleston claims to have found the boat in the 1970s. When the hull was located in 1995, the Hunley Commission was formed. This body is a joint effort of the National Park Service, the state of South Carolina, and the U.S. Navy. Author Clive Cussler has been interested in the recovery of the *Hunley* since 1981. Cussler's National Underwater Marine Agency became part of the effort to raise the *Hunley*.

On August 8, 2000, the *Hunley* rose from beneath the waters where it had been at rest since 1864. To the pealing of church bells and the firing of cannon, the submarine was loaded aboard a salvage vessel and moved to the Charleston Navy Yard, where conservation of the hull and the artifacts inside were to be carried out prior to putting the *Hunley* on public display.

By July 2001 the skeletal remains of the last crew of the *Hunley* had been located, entombed in the sediment that had filled the hull of the craft. Plans have been made to give the remains of the crew a military burial when the excavation of the hull is completed. One of the most exciting finds was a "lucky coin" carried by the commander of the *Hunley*. Lieutenant Dixon had been given the coin, a twenty-dollar gold piece, by his fiancée when he went away to the war. At

Shiloh, where Dixon served as an infantryman, the coin stopped a bullet that would otherwise have wounded him in the leg. This gold coin, dented by the bullet, was the one found with the remains of Lieutenant Dixon.

In the spring of 2000, the neglected and built-over graves of one of *Hunley*'s crews were discovered beneath the Citadel football stadium in Charleston. The cemetery in which they had originally been buried had been abandoned and forgotten. These men were buried with full military honors by Confederate reenactors on March 25, 2000.

A movie entitled *The Hunley* was released by Ted Turner and Warner Brothers on cable television in 1999.

A BATTLE OFF
THE COAST OF FRANCE

1864

Of all the fabled sea battles in United States history, few can rival the duel fought between the USS *Kearsarge* and the CSS *Alabama* off the harbor of Cherbourg, France, on June 19, 1864. This fight was to put the capstone on the legendary career of the Confederate commerce raider and was to enshrine in naval history the names of both ships and their commanders.

Captain Raphael Semmes of the *Alabama*, "Old Beeswax" to his crew in their private moments because of his highly waxed moustache, was a stern but fair disciplinarian and a fierce fighter. His British-built ship had gone far toward sweeping the Stars and Stripes from the seas over the past two years. Many American ship owners preferred to register their vessels under foreign flags rather than see them captured and burned by Semmes and the *Alabama*.

Commanding the *Kearsarge* was Captain John A. Winslow, a career naval officer whose service had won him steady promotion, but who had not shown any glimpse of genius or forcefulness of character. A competent, workmanlike officer, he did not have the flair and charisma needed to draw public attention to himself, nor did he need it. Prior to the battle, the *Kearsarge,* which had been built in 1861, had just had the benefit of a complete overhaul.

Alabama had been built under a secret contract negotiated by Captain James D. Bullock of the Confederate navy. The construction firm had been the Laird shipbuilders of Liverpool. Commissioned at sea on August 24, 1862, the ship cruised without pause until June 11, 1864. During that time fifty-seven merchant ships registered under the United States flag were captured and burned by the *Alabama.* Numerous other ships belonging to U.S. companies had been captured and released on bond because they were carrying cargoes belonging to neutral parties, or because Semmes used them to send his prisoners from other ships back home. In total, *Alabama* had sailed 75,000 miles while causing consternation in U.S. shipping circles.

The *Kearsarge* and *Alabama* were almost identical in size and in the number of crew members aboard. *Alabama* had a slight edge in the range of its armament because she carried a rifled cannon that fired a shell weighing one hundred pounds. The *Kearsarge's* main battery consisted of eleven-inch smoothbores that gave that ship an advantage in the total weight of shot fired at each broadside. Most of the *Alabama's* crew members were British, and even some of her officers were Europeans, while *Kearsarge* carried a crew, officers and men, who were all U.S. citizens.

At the end of his long two-year voyage, Captain Semmes took *Alabama* into the harbor at Cherbourg, France. He was contemplating spending several months in dry dock for a complete refit of his ship. The boilers of his vessel were quite rusty from using seawater for such a long period and could not carry a full head of steam. His officers and men needed rest after a campaign of almost two years' duration.

All over Europe, diplomats of the United States were alert for news of the *Alabama*. It was widely reasoned that she would seek haven in some port. When this happened, the plan was to use diplomatic pressure to deny *Alabama* aid, while naval forces were sent to fight the raider when she emerged from port. Surely, this time, the trap would snap shut on *Alabama*.

When news reached Captain Winslow of *Kearsarge* that *Alabama* was in port at Cherbourg, he immediately set sail for that place. On the way, he draped chains over the side of his ship in the vicinity of the engine room. These chains were then boxed in with light planks, and this addition was painted to match the rest of the hull. In the upcoming battle, this makeshift armor might give *Kearsarge* at least some protection for the vital parts of its hull.

Semmes received news of the imminent arrival of *Kearsarge* rather calmly. His ship was in no condition to run away from the enemy, so Semmes had only two options: He could abandon his ship to the French authorities, or he could fight. He chose the latter.

All day on Saturday, June 18, 1864, *Alabama* made ready to meet *Kearsarge*. All unnecessary furnishings and personal belongings were sent ashore, as were papers and official documents. Crew members who had no fighting role were left in charge of these goods, as were any men who admitted they could not swim.

On Sunday morning, June 19, escorted by a French warship that would make sure no fighting occurred inside French territorial waters, *Alabama* set out to do battle. Aboard *Kearsarge,* Captain Winslow was conducting church services when the foe was spotted. Final preparations were quickly made on both sides.

At a distance of about 1,200 yards, *Alabama* opened fire, taking advantage of the greater range of her rifled hundred-pounder. Both ships began a circling pattern that kept them starboard to starboard for the duration of the entire fight. This tactic gave *Alabama* her best chance of victory if she had speed enough to keep clear of *Kearsarge* and her gunnery were accurate enough to hit her opponent. Neither proved to be the case. *Kearsarge* not only was able to close in, but her gunners were much more accurate. *Alabama* fired 370 shots, scoring twenty-eight hits and wounding three men. *Kearsarge* fired 173 shots, almost all hitting home, riddling *Alabama*'s hull and killing or wounding forty-seven men.

After two hours of this pounding, *Alabama* was sinking under the feet of her crew. Semmes had all the wounded placed in a small boat and rowed to *Kearsarge,* while he and most of the crew took to the water. Boats from *Kearsarge* soon were passing among the swimmers, as was a British yacht called *Deerhound.* Many crew members, including Semmes, took refuge aboard *Deerhound,* where they were protected by the neutrality laws and did not become prisoners of war.

Less than half an hour after the "abandon ship" order was given, *Alabama* plunged to the bottom of the ocean, ending the career of the best-known commerce raider in the history of the United States.

In 1984 a French minesweeper, *Circe,* located the hull of the *Alabama.* A French naval team, led by Captain Max Guerout, examined the wreck and found it could not be raised. This site has been further explored by a nonprofit organization, the CSS Alabama Challenge. Among the artifacts recovered is the iron rim of the wheel of the ship.

On August 11, 2000, a five-ton, eight-foot-long cannon from the *Alabama* was delivered to the Warren Lasch Conservation Center in North Charleston, South Carolina, for cleaning and conservation. This cannon, which fired a thirty-two-pound ball, was recovered during the summer of 2000 at the location where the *Alabama* went down. The Lacsh Conservation Center now has the remains of two famous Confederate ships, the *Alabama* and the submarine *Hunley.*

HE DIED IN PLACE
OF HIS BROTHER

1864

Today a small, crumbling stone with an almost illegible inscription on the courthouse square at Fayetteville, Tennessee, is the only physical reminder of John R. Massey, a man who gave his life for his brother in the summer of 1864. But his story is one that deserves to be remembered as an act of sacrifice that happened in the Civil War.

July 15, 1864, was a bright, pleasant day in the county seat of Lincoln County, Tennessee, and life was about as good as it would get during the latter stages of the war. The gardens were beginning to produce early vegetables, and the monotony of the winter's diet of salted and dried food was being broken. The weather was turning hot, but that was to be expected in mid-southern Tennessee at that time of the year. The Confederate Army of Tennessee had been gone from the area for almost a year following the Tullahoma campaign, but as yet there was no permanent Union garrison in the village, only occasional visits from forage trains or a patrol out on a scout.

Fayetteville was in disputed territory. As the traffic along the

Nashville and Chattanooga Railroad increased in support of Sherman's campaign in North Georgia, an increasing number of Confederate cavalry and guerrilla units moved into the area around Fayetteville, attempting to interdict that traffic. These elusive units made life miserable for the Union garrisons guarding the railroad, so much so that one Union general, Eliazar A. Payne, decided to take drastic action.

Suddenly, the morning quiet of the July day in the county seat village of Fayetteville was shattered by gunfire. Union troops under General Payne rode into town, shooting left and right. Soon smoke was rising from numerous points as barns and outbuildings were set afire. Squeals of pigs and squawks of chickens blended with screams of terrified women as hostages were seized and dragged to the courthouse in the middle of the village. From the hostages assembled, these four were selected for execution: Thomas Massey, William Pickett, Franklin Burroughs, and Dr. J. W. Miller. Their lives would be spared only if someone in town gave information as to the whereabouts of a camp of Confederate cavalry or guerrillas. Franklin Burroughs had come to the courthouse to purchase a marriage license; he planned to wed the next day. William Pickett had come to town to purchase needed supplies at the general store. Thomas Massey was on his way to work when he was taken by the Union troops. Dr. Miller was not with the original group but was taken hostage later in the day. Years later Dr. Miller's son recalled the terrifying events of that day:

> *The day of the raid was a bright, sunny day. All nature was clad in its new garment of green. New Irish potatoes and English peas about ready for the table and our first "mess" appeared then. My brother and myself had*

*helped our mother get these vegetables from the garden,
she having apprised my father of the fact that "We are
going to have Irish potatoes and new peas for dinner."
This delighted him, as he was very fond of such things.*

Dr. Miller, it should be noted, had only recently been released
from Camp Chase, Illinois, having been held there as a prisoner
of war since the fall of Fort Donelson in February 1862. His son
continued:

*This pleasure and anticipation was soon swept away,
followed with despair, distress, mental anguish and van-
ishing hope—my father was arrested, charged with har-
boring bushwhackers, the same as Massey and the others.
The officers who took him in charge and carried him
off gave my mother no information as to his fate, despite
her pleadings for some knowledge of it, any more than to
say, "All damned bushwhacker harborers would be shot
and sent to hell." At 11:30 mother received notice that
all prisoners taken, charged just as mentioned, would be
killed at the same time, 3:00 that evening.*

General Payne had led his troops a short distance out of town to
the top of a nearby hill and halted them there for their midday dinner. The Miller family's cook had proceeded with the preparation for
their dinner despite all the confusion, and when Mrs. Miller learned
that her husband was still close to town, she prepared a plate of the
potatoes and peas and sent his son and a young African-American
slave to bring it to him. As his son described it:

*We found him sitting under a beech tree, surrounded
with six or eight men as a guard. Upon being handed
his dinner he courteously invited his guards to eat with
him, they refused but urged him to eat quickly since
they might move at any moment. While he was eating
General Payne rode up, surrounded by his staff, all on
fine horses, bright uniforms, sabers dangling. Payne
rode very near my father, not more than six feet away
and made a statement ever memorable to me, "You
G_d d___d grey-eyed bushwhacking sympathizer. I'll
have you shot at three o'clock this evening with Thomas
Massey and the other damned scoundrels." I grabbed
my father by the neck and begged for his life, but the
officers forced me away and told me to leave. When
my father hugged me to his bosom he said, "Good bye,
my little boy, I'll never see you again." No one but a
confiding child in a similar condition can realize the
awful agony of that moment.*

Soon after these scenes transpired, General Payne received a
visitor, John R. Massey. John had heard of the arrest of his brother,
Thomas, and of the impending execution. He had ridden into town
from his home west of Fayetteville and had gone to see General
Payne to plead for his brother's life. John made two points: His
brother Thomas had nothing to do with the Confederate army and
had probably been identified as a harborer of bushwhackers by a
neighbor who had a grudge against him; and, Thomas was the father
of a family of young children who would suffer a good deal, emo-
tionally and financially, by the loss of their father. General Payne

was unmoved by these arguments. Then John said, "If you must have Massey blood, take mine." Immediately, Payne agreed, releasing Thomas and arresting John in his place.

At three o'clock the Union soldiers fell into ranks with loaded rifles. Burroughs and Pickett were overcome by the situation and collapsed to the ground. John Massey reached down, seized each by the shirt collar and pulled them erect. "Kneel to God, but never to dogs like these!" Ripping open his shirt, Massey then said, "Do you so-called soldiers think you can hit the target at this range?" Gesturing at his heart, he concluded, "Then aim right here." A volley of shots rang out and the three collapsed. Burroughs still moved, so an officer ran him through with his saber. At dark, the young woman who was to have married Burroughs on the next day, Miss Molly Goodrich, ventured up the road to where the Yankees had paused, and there found the bodies of Massey, Pickett, and Burroughs lying as they had fallen. Dr. Miller, for reasons unknown, was taken some nine or ten miles farther toward Shelbyville and released. That night he was joyously reunited with his family.

All these deaths were tragic, and Payne had disobeyed the rules of war in taking hostages and murdering them. Most moving was the death of John R. Massey, a man innocent of any offense against the government of the United States, who volunteered to take the place of his brother in facing execution.

RAIDING REBELS ON THE RAMPAGE

1864

The wide prairie of Oklahoma, called the Cherokee Nation at the time of the Civil War, looked empty enough, but the wide grasslands were far from deserted. Out of sight in various folds and wrinkles in the earth were hundreds of soldiers. Some of these men wore Union blue; some wore ragged uniforms of Confederate gray. Some of these men were white, others were black, and many were copper-skinned Native Americans. And all of them were converging on the house of James L. Martin, which stood at the foot of a hill where the road from Fort Scott to Fort Gibson crossed Cabin Creek.

Major Henry Hopkins, one of the men in blue, was nervous. Under his protection were 200 army wagons, 5 ambulances, 40 artillery horses, and 1,253 mules. For the always needy, and sometimes hungry, Confederates, this large supply train was an opportunity to resupply at the expense of the North. Ninety wagons belonging to Union sutlers—civilians who supplied the armies with provisions—had joined his train, and these were especially tempting targets for Confederate raiders. The army wagons might be loaded with hardtack and bacon, shoes and overcoats, but the sutler wagons carried oysters and champagne, potted crabs and Rhine wine, cigars, beer, and cakes and pies, all the luxuries a soldier might want. To protect this vast collection of men, hardware, and horseflesh, Major Hopkins had only 260 men detached from the Second, Sixth, and Fourteenth Kansas cavalry regiments. Of this number only about half were mounted and mobile. The others rode in the wagons or plodded alongside the slow-moving vehicles. These Kansas regiments did not have a good reputation on the Confederate side of the border. The Kansas troops often referred to themselves as "Jayhawkers," and this sobriquet had become synonymous with murdering and looting in Missouri and Arkansas. Any clash with Confederates would be bloody, and neither side would expect to take many prisoners.

Stalking the prize drawn by the wagon teams were some two thousand Confederates. Brigadier General R. M. Gano commanded a band of cavalry from Texas, but the commander who received the major part of the attention was another brigadier, Stand Watie, a longtime leader of the Cherokee Nation and the first person of color to reach the rank of general in any American army. Eighty years before the U.S. Army granted a general's stars to an African American, the Confederacy had recognized the ability to command in a person of color.

Stand Watie led a brigade made up largely of Cherokees, but which also included significant numbers of Creeks and Seminoles. All these men had been recruited from the Indian Territory of Oklahoma, the area to which the U.S. government had forcibly moved them from their southeastern homelands—in states such as Georgia, North Carolina, and Florida—three decades earlier during the administration of Andrew Jackson.

Preparations for attacking the wagon train had begun a week earlier, on September 12, 1864, in the mountains of northwestern Arkansas and southwestern Missouri, where the Confederates had a stronghold. The Civil War had been especially intense and bitter in this area. A good argument could be made that the war did not begin at Fort Sumter in April 1861; instead the war began along the Kansas-Missouri border in 1854 and soon spilled over into Indian Territory. Long before secession occurred and armies were organized, bands of men had been raiding back and forth across the borders of pro-slavery Missouri and free-state Kansas, with the Indian Territory treated as a refuge by both sides. All too often the raids by either side were motivated by a desire to steal and despoil or to get revenge for a previous raid. Political issues became secondary to personal issues, and the troubled Kansas-Missouri-Oklahoma area, truly a cockpit of the war, would produce postwar outlaws such as the Youngers and the James Gang. Now, however, a purely military event was in the making.

Watie had met with Gano, and they had agreed to move in conjunction across the Arkansas River into Oklahoma. By September 16, Watie was attacking parties sent out by the U.S. Army to cut hay on the grasslands. Most of the Union troops in these parties were African Americans, members of the Seventy-ninth United States Colored Infantry, and many of them were former slaves. On the morning of September 18, a scout brought news of a more exciting nature. The wagon train had been sighted. Some reinforcements from the Third Cherokee Regiment (U.S.) had joined the train, and the entire party was headed toward the crossing of Cabin Creek, where the house of James Martin had been surrounded by a wooden palisade. If Watie had led only a cavalry raiding party, the wooded stockade might have been a major consideration, but accompanying him were six cannon, easily enough firepower to deal with any stockade.

During the night of September 18 to 19, Watie's men came up on the Union position. A long, gradual slope led down to the Union soldiers, who stood behind the logs of the stockade or lay behind piles of hay that curved from the little fort back to the creek. Within these lines the wagon train was parked in a crescent with the open side toward the creek.

Not content to wait for daylight, the men of Watie's command moved forward by the light of the moon. The men were accustomed to hunting at night, so fighting in darkness did not seem strange to them at all. Long before daylight, the Union position had been fully discovered, and Gano's men had gotten into place.

As the eastern sky began to turn gray, the mules of the wagon train started braying. It was time for them to be fed and watered! The noise caused Watie to fear that the wagons were being hitched up for an escape attempt, so he ordered Lieutenant Colonel John Vann, son of one of the principal chiefs of the Cherokee, to take his regiment to the rear of the Union position and cut off their retreat. Now that he could see, Watie placed his artillery to enfilade a portion of the Union line, including the stockade. Soon stockade timbers were flying through the air, and the piles of hay alongside the palisade had caught fire. This was more than the badly outnumbered Union troops could stand. Led by the civilian sutlers, the entire force turned to flee, but Vann's regiment was behind them and Watie's was in front.

In a few minutes the fight was all over. Fewer than a hundred Union soldiers and civilians escaped; just over a hundred were taken prisoner. The rest preferred to go down fighting. Many of the wagons were wrecked when their teams ran away, but 120 were taken intact, and these were loaded with as much as they could hold from the wreckage. Total losses among Watie's men were seven killed and sixteen wounded.

After completely clothing his men for the oncoming winter weather, Watie still had clothes for about two thousand men to be sent south. Also, he captured enough food and ammunition to carry his command through several months of campaigning. Truly, this had been a royal rampage for the Indian rebels, one of the most successful cavalry raids of the entire war—if not the most.

The command of General Stand Watie was the last Confederate land force to surrender in 1865.

THE PLOT TO DESTROY CHICAGO

1864

In the summer of 1864, the war did not seem to be going well for the Union, although it actually was. Armies under Grant and Sherman were slugging it out with Confederate adversaries in Virginia and Georgia, but the general public could see little progress toward an end to the war. What could be seen were the appalling Northern losses of almost one thousand men a day.

And 1864 was an election year. Lincoln was quite concerned about his chances for reelection and thought he could improve his political position by attracting pro-war Democrats to vote for him. To this end, Lincoln abandoned the Republican label, although he kept the Republican goals of ending slavery and winning the war, and asked a Democrat, Andrew Johnson of Tennessee, to be his running mate on the National Union ticket. Even so, more than once that summer Lincoln told his cabinet he did not expect to be returned to the White House.

In the North secret societies were rife, many of them opposed to the war and to Lincoln's reelection. Rumor exaggerated the numbers of members so that it could be believed that these societies were a major force. Also Confederate agents were active in the North. A small group of escaped Confederate prisoners of war had assembled in Canada and had made a successful raid to rob banks in St. Albans, Vermont. Another group of rebel escapees had seized two boats—the *Philo Parsons* and the *Island Queen*—on Lake Erie. These events caused widespread fears of a plot to attack various prison camps in the North, free the inmates, and then run riot across the North, burning cities and looting the countryside.

Amid all this fear and suspicion, the Democratic National Convention met in Chicago. Although many of the delegates, especially those from the Ohio River Valley, were suspected of being "copperheads," or sympathizers with the South, the initial meeting of the convention was routine, and the members even decided to adjourn until August 29, 1864. After some partisan political speeches, which included anti-Lincoln and antiwar language, the delegates went home to await the new date.

All this talk against Lincoln and against the war was too much for Colonel Benjamin Sweet to bear. The commandant of Camp Douglas had proven to be incompetent in leading troops in combat, but his new assignments in a rear area had made him the nervous guardian of almost eight thousand Confederates held in what had originally been a training camp for U.S. troops. Colonel Sweet was an ambitious man who was looking for a way to repair his tarnished reputation. In the vague rumors about disloyal Democrats and plots to free prisoners, he thought he had found the way to put his combat ineptitude behind him and to claim the mantle of a hero. Sweet found a ready ally in William A. Bloss, president of the company that owned the *Chicago Tribune,* and an ardent pro-war Republican. Between them, Sweet and Bloss were to create a conspiracy that would affect the lives of dozens of people alleged to be involved in a plot to destroy Chicago.

Using spies such as Isaiah Winslow Ayer, a rather shady character and ne'er-do-well, various Democratic clubs in the Chicago area were infiltrated, and anything that might be construed as unpatriotic was noted. It was discovered that a cache of weapons had been secreted at the home of Charles Walsh, who lived near Camp Douglas. Ostensibly, the weapons were for the protection of the Democrats of Chicago should the election campaign turn violent. The fact that the weapons were near the prison camp was enough for Sweet and Bloss to smell a rebel plot.

Joining the effort to gather information was John T. Shanks. Over the past three years, Shanks had joined, and then deserted, several Confederate military units. Posing as a destitute ex-Confederate, Shanks convinced the wife of Buckner S. Morris, a judge and prominent Democrat, to give him some old clothes and a small sum of money. This would become the basis for a charge of treason against Judge Morris and his wife.

Shanks also found out that Leger St. George Grenfell was in Chicago. This English soldier of fortune often posed as an aristocrat who had fought all over the world, and he had indeed recently been in Confederate service. Not an aristocrat at all, Grenfell was a dilettante and an adventurer who largely lived by his wits. His presence in Chicago seems to have been quite innocent because he had just spent several weeks hunting in southern Illinois.

These odd facts were, however, enough for Sweet and Bloss. On November 6, two days before the presidential election, Sweet ordered his soldiers to strike to prevent turmoil on Election Day, turmoil that might, he later said, include a breakout of the Camp Douglas prisoners.

Charles Walsh was arrested because of the cache of weapons at his house. Judge Buckner Morris was dragged from his bed at two o'clock in the morning and hauled off to Camp Douglas. Over one hundred men were arrested at various hotels across the city of Chicago, most of them hauled in simply because they were known to be Democrats. No sooner were the men arrested than Bloss ran a story in the *Tribune* that proclaimed their arrests were evidence of the existence of a plot to destroy the city and of the arrested ones' guilt. According to Bloss, he and Sweet had saved Chicago from a bloodbath, rescued Lincoln from defeat, and kept the nation from destruction. Democratic papers complained that the *Tribune* was printing rumors in an attempt to influence the election. At any rate, within a few days all charges had been dropped, except for those against eight men and one woman.

St. George Grenfell, who had been a Confederate officer, was portrayed as the leader of the proposed attack that would free the Camp Douglas prisoners and then ravage the city. Vincent Marma duke was the brother of a Confederate brigadier, which supposedly was evidence of his guilt. Benjamin Anderson, Charles Daniel, and George Cantrell had been in Southern ranks but had deserted. Judge and Mrs. Morris were anti-Lincoln and had been born in Kentucky. Charles Walsh had, on some occasions, had contact with Confederate secret agents, and two of his daughters had dated Daniel and Cantrell. Richard Semmes was arrested because he was thought to be the brother of Confederate Admiral Raphael Semmes. Actually, the two were in no way related.

Taken to Cincinnati for trial, all the defendants were brought before Major Henry L. Burnett of the judge advocate's office for the Cincinnati district. The very fact that the defendants were brought before a military judge raised serious questions about their trial. United States law did not allow for civilians to be tried by a military commission in areas where civil law was functioning. Colonel Sweet was so anxious to achieve a conviction and restore his tarnished reputation that he ignored the rule of law, and Lincoln did nothing to prevent the matter from continuing. After weeks of closed-door proceedings in which the defense lawyers had nothing against which to argue except accusations, the judge advocate delivered his decision. Marmaduke was released because nothing could be said against him. Semmes, however, was given three years in jail, apparently simply because of his name. Daniel had escaped his guards and was never heard from again. Anderson had committed suicide in prison, and this was accepted as proof of his guilt. Judge and Mrs. Morris were declared innocent, but they parted company and never lived together again as man and wife. Walsh received a sentence of five years in prison. Cantrell became insane and was committed to an asylum for life. Grenfell, the supposed ringleader, was sentenced to death. Apparently, Grenfell, being an Englishman at a time when diplomatic relations between the United States and Great Britain were strained, gave Sweet a chance to validate his charges of a plot via a death sentence no one would challenge.

Sweet got his wish—promotion to brigadier general—while Bloss saw the *Tribune* become the preeminent Republican organ in the Midwest. Was there a plot to free Confederate prisoners from Camp Douglas and to attack Chicago? Some loose talk in barrooms and in the meetings of romantic secret societies probably did take place. It is the opinion of most historians today that Colonel Sweet saved Chicago from a "plot" that existed only in his and Bloss's minds. It seems that lives were ruined and people died to satisfy the ambitions of two political hacks.

Grenfell's death sentence was commuted to life in prison, and he was sent to Dry Tortugas, a maximum security prison for the most desperate criminals. In 1868 he died in an escape attempt.

A SAD HOMECOMING

1864

There it was! He could see it! His home was in sight, not two miles away across a completely open field. Captain Theodoric "Tod" Carter had not seen his home or his family for more than three and a half years, but now he could almost touch the house he called home. But across the very lawn of his home, less than thirty feet from the doorway, was a line of breastworks bristling with cannon and lined with Yankee soldiers. Home might be close, but it was going to take work to get there.

Tod Carter was used to work. He had been only nineteen years old when the war began, but he had enlisted with his brother, Moscow, and other boys from the town of Franklin and its surrounding area in what would become the Twentieth Tennessee Infantry. Since those early days of the war, the Twentieth Tennessee had traveled far, from Bristol, Virginia, to Baton Rouge, Louisiana; from Fishing Creek, Kentucky, to Atlanta, Georgia. Now they had come home to Franklin, Tennessee. Those that were left had come home. There had been 850 of them when they left for their training camp in June

1861. Now, on this last day of November 1864, there were fewer than 200 of them left. Many were lying in shallow graves all across five states; others had been sent home, their bodies shattered by wounds. A few, like Tod's brother, had been captured and exchanged and sent home on parole. A few days earlier those who were left had marched past a sign someone had erected just inside the Tennessee state line. A FREE HOME OR A GRAVE, it read. "Well," thought Tod, "maybe it won't be so bad. It's almost dark, only an hour of daylight left. Those Yankees want to get to Nashville, especially after the scare we gave them yesterday. As soon as it gets dark, they will skedaddle, and we can move in to Franklin. There's not enough time left for a battle today."

Little did Tod Carter know about what was going on only a few hundred yards away at Confederate army headquarters. There the commanding general, John Bell Hood, was having an angry confrontation with his subordinate officers. Twenty-four hours earlier, at Spring Hill, Tennessee, Hood's Confederates had been closing in on the Union force of General James Schofield. An advance of a half-mile or less would have cut the Union line of retreat to Franklin and Nashville, and there were almost no Union soldiers blocking that half-mile gap. Yet because of fatigue, darkness, and confusion, that gap had not been closed, and Schofield's entire army had escaped. When General Hood found out what had happened, he blamed everyone but himself, even calling his soldiers and their commanders cowards. Now late in the day as it was, Hood was determined to punish his army, to "make them fight." Two years earlier Hood would have led the attack himself, but he had lost an arm and a leg in combat and was no longer capable of leading an assault. But he certainly could order one!

So the orders came and the Confederate Army of Tennessee began to fall into line along the slopes of Winstead Hill. Had anyone thought of it and cared to make comparisons, this was going to be bigger than the Confederate attack at Gettysburg. "Pickett's Charge" involved about twelve thousand men; here nearly twenty thousand lined up for the assault. Pickett's men advanced over a mile of cleared ground; Hood's army would cover two miles. Pickett had the protection of an artillery barrage; Hood had not a single cannon on the field.

In the waning light of the November afternoon, Tod Carter took his place in the line. Although currently carried on the roll as acting quartermaster, he knew every man would be needed, and as he had always done, he took his place in the ranks.

Two miles away at their home, Tod's parents waited also. They were certain that Tod was with the army, but they had no idea where his unit was. They did know they were going to be in the middle of a fierce battle, and that the upper levels of their comfortable, though not elaborate, farmhouse were no place to be at such a time. Gathering up his farm workers (once slaves but now working for wages) and as many of his neighbors as wanted a place of refuge, Fountain Carter led his family into the basement. There they would spend the next eight hours praying and crying, as the hell of combat swirled around them.

On Winstead Hill the "Forward, march" order came, and with bands playing and flags waving, the Army of Tennessee moved to the attack. Awaiting them, the Union troops of General Schofield stood to their weapons and watched them come.

About three hundred yards in front of their main line, some Union officer had placed two small brigades to hold a slight rise. These men looked with growing concern at the gray ranks steadily tramping toward them. Artillery shells exploded over the heads of the rebels and men went down, but the ranks closed up and the attack moved on. It was obvious, that gray wave was going to roll right over them! Now the rebs were only yards away, now they were pausing to take aim. Then a sheet of fire flashed from the leveled rifle barrels, and almost without firing a shot in return, the survivors of the two Union brigades turned to run.

"After 'em, boys. Stay on their tails. Go into the Yankee lines with 'em." Such was the rallying cry from every Confederate officer—Tod Carter with the rest. The retreating Yankees would block the fire from their friends behind the breastworks, and the Confederates could jump over the fortifications with the fugitives.

So it was that the two armies came face to face, only the width of a small pile of dirt and logs between them. And so it was they stood and fought for the next eight hours. On both sides the living stood on top of the dead and wounded to shoot, stab, and club their opponents only an arm's length away.

Sometime after midnight the fighting wound down, and the Union army slipped away toward Nashville. Five Confederate generals lay dead along with hundreds of their men, while thousands more were wounded.

At first light Fountain and Moscow Carter came out of their basement. Dead men of both armies littered their yard. Every room of their house was crammed with wounded. Then one of the farm workers approached.

"Mister Carter, young Mister Tod is lying in the vegetable garden yonder. He's alive, but he's shot all to pieces."

Quick as they could, the father and the brother found helpers and ran to the rear of their property. There they found the still-breathing body of Tod Carter. He had been wounded in six places. Gently, he was carried to his own room and placed in the bed where he had slept as a boy. As soon as they could, surgeons dressed his wounds and performed an operation to repair some of the internal damage. But the case was beyond their skills. Later that night Tod

Carter gained consciousness and spoke to his mother and sisters, but by daylight he was dead.

Tod Carter had come home, but only to die.

Today most of the Franklin battlefield has been swallowed up by urban growth. There is a small park on Winstead Hill from which one can view the ground of the Confederate advance and the Union defense. The home of Tod Carter is a museum, the Carter House Museum, and is one of three historic homes where the battle of Franklin is interpreted for visitors.

HE KEPT THE BOYS IN BLUE SINGING

1865

"Confound that man! I hate him and I despise what he has done to this war," ranted General William Tecumseh Sherman. The general was not talking about an opponent in the Southern army, nor was he referring to anyone associated with the Confederacy. The target of Sherman's ire was Henry Clay Work, the most popular of all songwriters in the United States, the author and composer of "Marching Through Georgia." Although the song celebrated Sherman's greatest success of the entire war, its strains greeted Sherman every time he made a public appearance and he had come to despise the tune and its creator.

Regardless of Sherman's opinion, the brain and the pen of Henry Clay Work contributed to the victory of the Union. Work had kept the boys in blue singing, giving a boost to morale when it was most needed. Indeed, Work has often been called "The War Poet." "Marching Through Georgia" became his most popular song, partly because it was written in 1865 when the war was almost over and its words could celebrate the imminent Union victory. That event would bring the "jubilee," the time of celebration for the preservation of the Union and the end of slavery. The song allowed the Northern public to look back with pride and joy on what had been accomplished instead of anticipating sacrifices that lay ahead. For that reason, the tune would be popular in the North for years after the war as Union veterans gathered in reunions. It was at one of these postwar gatherings that Sherman burst out with his opinion of the song.

Henry Clay Work gave more to the Union cause than a triumphal song of celebration of work done. He also wrote music to encourage the nation as it was going into the war, composed anthems to keep spirits up when the outcome of the war was in doubt, and made soldiers and civilians laugh during dark, sad times. Work had put his heart into the war effort.

Growing up in Middletown, Connecticut, in the 1830s, Work had been named for a statesman of his day who was a champion of the concept of national union, Henry Clay. Work's father, Alanson, was an antislavery activist who was sentenced to a term in prison in Illinois because he violated the law by assisting runaway slaves. This family background made Work dedicated to ideas that would become part of the Union cause. As a young man, Henry Clay Work was apprenticed to a music printer. In 1853 he wrote his first published song, "We Are Coming, Sister Mary." This song was frequently used by the Christy Minstrels as part of their show since it was written in a pseudo-Negro dialect. The song tells the story of a group of mourners preparing for a funeral.

The outbreak of the Civil War found Work in Chicago, where he was employed by the music publishing company of George Root. Work brought to his employer a song titled "Kingdom Coming," also written in dialect, in which a slave pokes fun at his master for running away when the only threat is the distant smoke of a Union gunboat. The slave narrator concludes that "the kingdom is coming and the year of Jubilo." This humorous song provided a jab at Southern aristocrats and provided subtle support for the abolitionist point of view that the war should be directed against slavery, a view not held by many people in the North at the time. The song quickly became a hit. Later in the war, Work's tune "Babylon Is Fallen" urged black men to enlist in the Union army.

The nineteenth-century audiences liked sentimental entertainment, and Work provided that, too. "Sleeping for the Flag" reminded listeners that many who had volunteered to fight for the flag were now sleeping in an unmarked grave under a Southern tree. "Little Major" narrated the final moments of a drummer boy, mortally wounded in battle, who is left to die on the field because the stretcher bearers do not think it worth their attention to carry a boy to the field hospital.

Work knew how to make people laugh and he understood that humor was an essential quality for good soldiers. In "Grafted into the Army," Work pokes fun at an ignorant lad whose family laments that he has been "grafted" into the army when his draft notice arrives. "Corporal Schnapps" is written in a broken-English dialect that lampoons the speech of many German immigrants who enlisted to fight for the Union.

Although Work was a prolific writer, turning out dozens of songs on subjects ranging far beyond the themes of the Civil War, he was a careful craftsman. He wrote slowly, spending days working over the rhyme schemes and carefully selecting each word. It was rumored that Work never wrote down his songs but actually sat at a linotype machine, composing words and music and setting the type all at the same time. Work enjoyed this legend, as any celebrity would enjoy having people talk about his skills, but he never claimed that he worked in this fashion.

None of these songs ever matched "Marching Through Georgia." Set to a tune that evokes the image of long lines of men swinging along in easy route step, the song uses a format that has become a classic of American popular music—a verse followed by a chorus whose words contain a "hook," a repeated phrase that sums up the main idea of the song. In "Marching Through Georgia," there are humorous references to Union soldiers foraging for sweet potatoes and turkeys, comments about the welcome offered Union soldiers by the ex-slaves, and allusions to pro-Union Southerners and easy victories over rebels. The swath of destruction left by Sherman is called a "thoroughfare for freedom." No wonder the song was wildly popular in the North for years as old veterans gathered, even though its repetition drove Sherman to distraction. No wonder the song never caught on in the South.

Despite the popularity of his wartime songs, Work had a difficult time earning a living for himself and his family. Music was not copyrighted at that time, and Work had to depend on direct sales of his sheet music and the honesty of printers for his income. Although he wrote many songs that today would be labeled "hits," he was often on the brink of poverty.

Today, except among students of the Civil War, Work's songs are largely unknown, although Princeton University uses the tune of "Marching Through Georgia" for its "fight song." The use of ethnic dialect in many of his songs makes many people today hesitant to sing or even to listen to Work's tunes. Despite his contribution of many war songs to the Union cause, ironically it is a postwar song by Work, "My Grandfather's Clock," that survived to the present. This tune has become a folk music standard, often performed by bluegrass musicians. In 2004 the R&B group Boyz II Men recorded their take on this song. Work was inducted into the Songwriters Hall of Fame in 1970. Sometimes, we still sing the tunes of Henry Clay Work.

LINCOLN'S FAVORITE SONG

1865

He was tired, very, very tired. But he had reason to be. For four years, excepting only three days, he had led a nation at war. There had been dark days when it appeared that the war would be lost and the nation permanently divided. Much blood had been shed and treasure spent, but now the end had come. That very morning—April 9, 1865—at a dusty crossroads in Virginia named Appomattox Court House, the largest Confederate army, the Army of Northern Virginia, had agreed to surrender. The Union commander, Ulysses S. Grant, had been generous in his terms and the Confederate leader, Robert E. Lee, had accepted. Grant had required only that each Confederate soldier, from the commanding general to the lowliest private, sign a pledge not to fight anymore against the government of the United States. On turning in their weapons, they were free to go home. Officers could keep their swords, and any man who claimed a horse or mule from the army wagon trains could take the animal home to begin spring plowing.

Abraham Lincoln liked those terms. No arrests, no detention camps, no trials for treason. There was no need for revenge, although many people in the North wanted just that. But the war had lasted long enough, the president felt, and now it was time for healing.

When the telegram from the fighting front had arrived at the War Department in Washington, D.C., the news had flashed across the capital city like a lightning bolt. All day people had been surging about the streets in celebration, and there had been an endless stream of people thronging the White House, all wanting to shake the president's hand and exult in the end of the war. But Lincoln didn't feel much like celebrating; his emotion was more like sorrow.

"But, Mr. President, we've won! The rebels are crushed. We have them under our boots now." How many had said words like that?

Yes, they had won, but at what a cost? Hundreds of thousands dead of illness and in combat. A great part of the country devastated by four years of war. And the bitterness! Given what he was hearing from the victor about the South, what must the losing side be saying about the North? How long would it take to get over all that bitterness? Those who were exulting were wrong. The people of the South must not be treated as hated rebels and held down with a boot on their necks. They must be welcomed back to the fold as fellow Americans.

He had tried to get some of that spirit of reconciliation across the preceding month at his inaugural in March. "With malice toward none, with charity for all," he had said in his speech. Even in his plan for reconstruction, he had tried to be gentle. Only 10 percent of the population of a seceded state had to swear an oath of future loyalty before they could form a state government. As soon as that government abolished slavery, then that state could hold elections for senators and congressmen and its reconstruction would be over. Lincoln only hoped some zealots in Congress did not cause trouble by pressing for revenge against the South. A lengthy reconstruction process would create bitterness and keep alive needless hostility.

A lengthy reconstruction was just what some members of Congress wanted, and they belonged to his own Republican party. Just the previous November the Congress had passed the Wade-Davis Bill, which set up a way for the states to reenter the Union. Lincoln had been able to pocket veto that bill, and a good thing, too, he thought. In contrast to his proposal that 10 percent of the population of a seceded state swear to be loyal in the future, the Wade-Davis Bill had demanded that a majority of the population of a state swear that it had always been loyal to the United States government. Of course that would mean that the wartime generation would have to die out and a new generation, born after the war, would have to reach adulthood before any Southern state could begin the process of reconstruction. During that period of fifty or so years, there would be military occupation and martial law throughout the former Confederacy. "If a person were not already a rebel," thought Lincoln, "that prospect of lengthy military occupation would make them one." No, healing and reunion—that had to be the order of the day.

Of course celebration was appropriate. The war was over and the Union had won. Of course relief was appropriate; the dying was almost over and the healing could begin. Lincoln wanted to participate in the celebration, but he wanted to promote the healing. All day long these two ideas ran through Lincoln's mind: celebration and healing.

That evening, as the sun was sinking and the April sky was beginning to be spangled with stars, a crowd formed on the South Lawn of the White House. Soon a brass band joined them. Most people in the crowd waved a flag or held aloft a flaming torch. To keep up their enthusiasm, the band played a medley of patriotic songs popular in the North. No one gave a signal, but the entire crowd surged up to the entrance of the president's house.

"Come out, Mr. Lincoln, come out!"

"We want a speech."

"Speech, speech!"

Slowly curtains were drawn back and a window was opened. Now everyone could see the familiar tall, lanky form of the president. Quiet swept over the crowd. He spoke:

> *Friends, we have come to the end of a long and terrible war. Not a home in our land but has been touched by it. Some of the results of that war were much to be desired. The Union has been preserved and slavery has been ended.*
>
> *Other results have been necessary but unfortunate. Devastation has been wrought upon part of our land. Bitterness and hostility are abroad in both the North and the South. On this night let us celebrate the good, and let us also begin to bind up the wounds of war.*
>
> *Now, as my contribution to the healing and to the celebration I want the band which is with you to play a song. It has always been my favorite song, and now I can hear it played again. From tonight this song belongs to all of us, North as well as South. Let the band play "Dixie."*

And it did.

HE BROKE INTO A
PRISONER OF WAR CAMP

1865

Sawney Webb had seen quite enough of war, but war was not through with him. Being a man of strong principles who would keep his word, no matter what, he would not merely walk away from the war, although he was about to walk away from a prisoner of war camp and into the heart of New York City.

Webb was a student at the University of North Carolina when the war began. He was somewhat shy around the other students and was not attracted to the camaraderie that army life promised. Also, he was rather uncertain about secession, but when North Carolina did leave the Union, Webb went with his state. Soon he was a private in the Fifteenth North Carolina Infantry. Better educated than many of the troops and with an appealing personality, he soon found himself chosen to be a sergeant. Several of the soldiers who were illiterate asked Webb to write letters home for them. This was a high mark of confidence, as was the position given him as the man who divided the rations. This was a task everyone scrutinized carefully to make sure each person got a fair share. Clearly, it was almost impossible to please everyone, but Webb won a reputation for absolute fairness.

For several months the war brought merely boredom for the Fifteenth North Carolina, but action came thick and heavy when the Peninsula campaign of 1862 began. The regiment was in the assault on Malvern Hill, the last of the Seven Days' Battles around Richmond. The Union army had taken up a formidable position on a hill that rose abruptly above the surrounding swampy countryside. This naturally strong position was reinforced by over one hundred pieces of artillery and by gunboats firing from the James River. The Confederate attack was hopeless. Among the many casualties was Sawney Webb, who was severely wounded in the right shoulder.

While recuperating from his wounds, Webb was invited to teach at a local academy and was thus introduced to the career he would follow after the war. Webb found he had a real talent for teaching, and he enjoyed a bond of sympathy with the young men under his supervision. He always told them the truth and expected them to do the same with him. He always kept his word and expected his students to do likewise. The shoulder wound was slow to heal, and his convalescent leave was extended through the rest of 1862 and 1863. By 1864 the South's need for men was pressing. Webb was called back to duty, this time with the Second North Carolina Cavalry.

Again, Webb's education and personality served him well, and he soon rose in rank from private to captain. He also took place in the bloody series of battles from the Wilderness to Petersburg. Although he saw the South constantly growing weaker, with all hopes of independence fading, he felt honor-bound to live up to the oath he had taken to serve to the end.

That end seemed to come quite close on April 3, 1865. The Confederate lines around Petersburg had been broken on April 2, and the army was retreating west. At Amelia Courthouse, Virginia, Webb and several other men from his regiment were captured. Now came a severe test of character. All those who would declare themselves deserters from the rebel ranks could go free, but those who refused that label would become prisoners of war. Webb chose the latter course. Eight days later Sawney Webb was in a prison called Castle Garden at the Battery on the tip of Manhattan Island. In his pocket was seventy cents, the change from some money a relative had managed to get to him while he was on his way north. Life in the prison camp was crude and hard. Rations were not plentiful, and the Union guards made no attempt to issue them fairly. Webb later recalled that the food was simply dumped into the prison compound, and the men had to scramble for what they could get. A gang of larger, stronger men usually took all they wanted for themselves, leaving the weaker men little to eat. Finally, the prisoners organized themselves into a self-governing body, attacked the gang, and beat them up. Because he had once been the officer to issue rations for the Fifteenth North Carolina, Webb was placed in charge of food distribution and saw that all prisoners received equal amounts, even the former gang members.

On June 7, 1865, Webb saw that no guard was watching the river side of the prison yard. In that day and age, very few people knew how to swim, but Webb had learned as a boy. During his army service he found swimming a good way to keep clean, and the exercise helped him maintain flexibility in his wounded shoulder. Seizing the opportunity, he slipped into the water and swam to shore. Without anyone noticing him, he quickly disappeared into the thick traffic of the New York streets. Not far away was the famous Barnum's

Museum, which he had always wanted to see, so in he went. After looking at several of the exhibits, he was startled when a boa constrictor suddenly confronted him in the next glass case. Stumbling backward, Webb crashed into a display. A crowd, including Federal soldiers, gathered.

"Those are Confederate buttons on your coat," said one of the soldiers.

"Yes," replied Webb, telling the truth, as he always did. "I am an escaped prisoner of war." The crowd broke up in laughter, thinking Webb was part of the show being put on by Barnum for their entertainment. Next Webb went to a theater and bought a seat in the gallery. Suddenly, a loud voice exclaimed, "There is a rebel sitting beside me." Again a crowd gathered, and again it dissolved in laughter when Webb announced that he was an escaped prisoner. Many of the women were especially amused that a person of so slight a build would be mistaken for a soldier.

Hungry after his adventures, Webb went to a restaurant, but having only a dime left of his money, he ordered ten cents worth of bread. The waitress brought him a huge meal.

"Honey, I'm from Georgia and by the sound of your voice, you ain't no Yankee. Eat all you want," she said.

By midnight Webb was tired and sleepy, so he walked back to Castle Garden. Only a dim light illuminated the open gate and the guard's back was turned. Webb walked through the gate and a few feet into the compound, then immediately turned around so he was facing the gate.

"Guard," he called, "why can't I go visit the town?"

"You damned rebel, get to your barracks," the suddenly alert guard yelled. And with a smile, Webb went. He had just broken out of and back into a prison camp.

Author's note: Following the Civil War, Sawney Webb completed his education and moved to Tennessee. There he founded a now internationally known preparatory school, The Webb School, in Bell Buckle, Tennessee. The student body of The Webb School currently has enrolled students from across the United States and has a strong international presence.

BOM DIA, Y'ALL

1865

On November 9, 1865, a wagon train left the little community of Spring Hill in Navarro County, Texas. Its ultimate destination was Brazil. Riding in one of the wagons was ten-year-old Sarah Bellona Smith who, in 1935, would recount the adventures and exploits of some of the more than four thousand Southerners who left the United States in voluntary exile to go to Brazil. In their new country they hoped to make new lives for themselves in a land of rich soil and a climate similar to that of Dixie. They knew they would be welcomed there because the ruler of Portugal, Dom Pedro II, was actively seeking settlers for this Portuguese colony. Dom Pedro hoped these settlers would introduce cotton farming to Brazil, allowing that country to become the new source of fiber for the British textile mills. These rebel immigrants were just the catalyst needed to make that dream a reality.

Rumors were rife in Texas in the autumn of 1865. Some said the Midwest was about to secede from the Union and form a trade alliance with the South, along the axis of the Mississippi River. Others said all ex-Confederates were to be arrested and executed. Some things were quite clear: There was no money, the infrastructure of the economy was destroyed, and there appeared to be no immediate prospect of a return to economic or social stability. The Congress of the United States had adjourned in April 1865, following the funeral of Abraham Lincoln. During the intervening months, from April to November, Andrew Johnson had attempted to guide the nation through some process of reconstruction. But the new president was in a weak position. He was a Democrat who had run for vice president on a ticket headed by a Republican. Now neither party trusted him. Although Johnson had proposed his own plan for reconstruction, Congress was sure to disagree when that body reconvened. Against this background of uncertainty, the wagon train moved south from Spring Hill, Texas.

To young Sarah this was all a lark. For two weeks she and her family camped along the road as they traveled toward Houston. Almost every day another family joined them, and there were more children to play with, new friends to be made. On reaching Houston, quite a crowd was found to be awaiting the party that included Sarah, and soon there was another new experience for the little girl. Loading all their goods into freight cars, the families climbed aboard atop their furniture and set off for Galveston by train. Then came the truly great adventure: boarding a sailing ship for Brazil.

Adults seemed to settle into the trip's routine only slowly, but the children quickly accommodated themselves to life aboard a ship. The voyage to Cuba, the first stage of the journey, took thirty-three days, thirty-two of them calm, but the last a day of a violent storm that wrecked the ship and left the voyagers castaways on the shores of a foreign land.

Sarah and her traveling companions were befriended by a Cuban plantation owner who helped the would-be colonists salvage most of their goods from the wrecked ship. Finally, after many days of work under the Cuban sun, the party proceeded on their way to Brazil by going to New York City! The group spent a month in New York, seeing the sights and being seen by the curious. Quite a lot of sympathy was expressed for the plight of the exiles-in-making during their stay in New York. There had been a strong streak of pro-Southern feeling in the city even during the war years because of business ties with Dixie. The economy of New York City revolved around textiles, and textile manufacturers needed cotton from the South. The group spent a pleasant month in the city before sailing for Rio de Janeiro aboard a steamer. There, Dom Pedro II received the colonists and welcomed them to their new homeland. A few days later they were on their way up the Juquia River to find land on which to settle.

What a trip Sarah remembered that to have been! Whole families, with all their goods, packed themselves into large dugout canoes propelled upriver by two Brazilian Indians in each canoe. The strange trees, the unknown flowers, the exotic birds made the trip a time both of excitement and terror as they moved into an unknown land. On one occasion they were caught in a rainstorm so fierce that they could not see the banks of the river and feared they would all drown. On another occasion the Indians had to pole the canoes up and over a cascading rapids fifty feet long, with a drop of almost four feet.

August 11, 1866, ten months after leaving Texas, Sarah and her family arrived at their new home. Now they were true pioneers, clearing land, planting crops, erecting shelter, and learning to live in a new place. Their diet changed, too, as the traditional southern dishes of pork, peas, and corn bread were replaced by bananas, manioc root, and rice.

Some things, however, did not change. Portuguese remained for Sarah a second language; she spoke it with the speech patterns of her native South. In a Catholic country the colonists were Protestants, and soon their settlements were dotted with Presbyterian, Methodist, and Baptist churches.

Further, agricultural innovations were introduced by these settlers. Sarah recalled how the moldboard plow replaced the hoe as the primary instrument of cultivation, and how her family astounded their Brazilian neighbors by having a steel-tired buckboard wagon instead of an ox cart. Soon these were being copied throughout the land. All this allowed the colony to put down roots and even to prosper while engaging in a cultural exchange with their new homeland.

Author's note: Several groups of colonists came from the postwar South to Brazil. They came from almost all of the ex-Confederate states, and many of the colonists experienced a journey much like that described by Sarah Smith. In all, as many as four thousand "Confederados" would emigrate to Brazil. Gradually, the survivors of the various groups concentrated around the town of Santa Barbara in the state of Sao Paulo.

Each year a festival is held at the Campo Church and campground near Santa Barbara. The Confederate battle flag waves above young men in gray uniforms, while young women don crinolines and antebellum-style dresses. Fried chicken and watermelon heap trestle tables and the southernmost Confederates greet each other with "*Bom dia, y'all.*"

The Sons of Confederate Veterans hosts an annual exchange program for young people from Dixie to visit their Confederado cousins in Brazil and for those cousins to come to the land once home to their ancestors.

Bom dia is Portuguese for "good day."

THE ANGEL OF THE BATTLEFIELD—
CLARA BARTON

1865–68

Gary Scott, chief historian of the National Park Service in the Washington, D.C., area gasped as he entered the attic of the old run-down building that was on the verge of being demolished. It was not the stifling heat nor the stale air that caused him to gasp, but instead the sight of all the artifacts that littered the space. Faded newspapers, copies of government reports, a hat, bits of rugs, two boxes filled with men's clothing, and over two hundred letters from the years immediately following the Civil War all vied for space. But what proved to be the most valuable relic was a small tin sign bearing the words:

MISSING SOLDIERS OFFICE

3RD STORY ROOM 9

MISS CLARA BARTON

Here was a missing piece from the puzzle of the past.

Much of the work performed by Clara Barton during the Civil War is well known and well documented. She had come to Washington some years before the war in order to make a change of career. For eighteen years she had been a teacher in her hometown of Oxford, Massachusetts, but looking for a new outlet, she had gotten a job at the Patent Office. There was a rather strong prejudice at the time against women working in offices, and this prejudice caused her employment to be rather uncertain. She had absorbed a fierce patriotism from her father, and when the Civil War began, she started to look for an active role in the conflict.

The opportunity for activity presented itself when a regiment from her home state, the Sixth Massachusetts Infantry, became the first regiment to arrive to defend the capital. Some men from the unit were injured in a clash with a mob in Baltimore, and many others had lost all their personal possessions by the time they arrived at their temporary quarters in the capitol chambers. Clara Barton immediately set to work collecting personal items and food with which to supplement the government rations of "her boys." She also began a campaign of letter writing to friends across the North, including letters meant for publication in newspapers. Soon boxes and packages were flowing into Washington, so many that Clara had to move to a larger apartment to have room to store the goods.

The first battle near Manassas, Virginia, along the banks of Bull Run, brought another side of the war home to Clara Barton. Hundreds and hundreds of wounded men came streaming into Washington, many of them hungry and still caked with blood. While doing all she could to relieve suffering, Clara could only imagine how much worse conditions must be in the field. Throughout the rest of 1861 and into 1862, Clara collected supplies from supporters throughout the North. In May and June wounded soldiers again began to pour into Washington from the fighting in the Shenandoah Valley and, later, from around Richmond.

More than ever, Clara wanted to be in the field, but she was restrained by two factors. The army did not want her because they feared she would be more trouble than help, and Clara was hesitant to challenge the social customs of the day that prevented women from doctoring men. "Nice" women were not supposed to deal with blood or bodily waste or with nudity. However, she was soon to overcome both of these restraints. As the war moved back into the Washington area in August 1862, the need for nurses became so great that the army actually offered assistance to Clara in her efforts. During the rest of that year, all of 1863, and into 1864, she was often found near the front lines, sometimes under artillery fire, helping those most in need of her aid. Although not a trained nurse, she administered first aid until surgeons could care for the wounded. Because it sometimes took doctors several days to reach all the wounded, this initial care saved many who otherwise simply would have bled to death. Once the battlefield had been cleared, Clara eased the lot of convalescents by distributing small luxuries, such as jelly or hot soup.

However, the nature of the war was changing. As the great battle summer of 1864 wore along, the Union army began to put more and more pressure on volunteers such as Clara Barton to conform to a pattern that the army laid down. The army felt that a uniform approach to hospital care would concentrate resources where they were needed most and would bring order to the volunteer efforts. Clara Barton was too much of an individualist and had too strong an ego to squeeze herself into a mold. As a result, she was slowly squeezed out of the army hospitals.

Disappointed that her work was not more appreciated and depressed by the deaths of so many Massachusetts friends and former pupils, Clara was searching for the next phase of her life when President Abraham Lincoln asked her to help organize an effort to find out what had happened to the approximately sixty-two thousand Union soldiers missing in action. This was a daunting task. Civil War soldiers did not wear dog tags. If a soldier was wounded and sent to a hospital, he might be surrounded by strangers. If he died, his grave would be marked "unknown." Even if buried by friends, such temporary grave markers as comrades were able to erect were not likely to survive the war, and memories about who died where quickly faded. And if a soldier's body was buried by the enemy, it was usually in a mass grave. Confederate records listing the deaths of captured Union wounded or deaths in prisoner of war camps were often destroyed in the various conflagrations that marked the end of the war. The Missing Soldiers Office would not have much to work with. Letters began to go out to friends and to newspapers asking for any information about soldiers who had not come home. Soon letters were flowing back and forth, sixty-three thousand asking for information about missing loved ones, and forty-two thousand replies going back. One visitor to Room 9 was Dorence Atwater, a former prisoner of war at the camp near Andersonville, Georgia. While a prisoner there, Atwater had been assigned to work in the records office, where he kept a list of the Union soldiers who died in the camp and where they were buried. Atwater had managed to hold on to a list of those deceased, a list with thirteen thousand names on it. By the time her Missing Soldiers Office shut down in 1868, Clara Barton had revealed the fate of about twenty-two thousand missing Union soldiers.

The end of the Civil War was not the end of Clara's service. In 1881 she was successful in overseeing the foundation of the National Society of the Red Cross, an organization of which she would serve as president for the next twenty-three years. Until her death in 1912 at the age of ninety, she remained the "Angel of the Battlefield."

Clara's office, discovered in 1997, is now being renovated and may yet yield more clues about the activities of this remarkable woman and her search for soldiers missing in action.

UNITED IN DEATH

1891

The old man stood, hat in hand, as the cold February rain ran down his balding head, soaking his neck and shoulders. The gloomy February day was typical of New York weather, but that day in 1891 seemed especially cheerless to thousands of Union veterans who were accompanying the coffin of their wartime leader, William Tecumseh Sherman, to the train station for the trip to St. Louis, where he would be buried.

One of the mourners leaned forward. "Put your hat on, general. You will catch your death."

"No, sir," the general replied. "If I were in his place and he were standing here in mine, he would not put on his hat."

The general was Joseph Eggleston Johnston. In the summer of 1864, he and Sherman, between them commanding almost two hundred thousand men, had maneuvered and battled against each other all over North Georgia. Then they had been enemies.

Sherman and Johnston had both been in the "Old Army" in the years prior to the Civil War. During the Mexican War, Johnston had seen considerable combat, while Sherman had been given assignments behind the lines. Following the war with Mexico, both men had seen service in the territory the United States had taken from Mexico, Sherman being posted in California as adjutant to the department commander, and Johnston in Missouri, Kansas, and as an emissary to Mexico at Vera Cruz.

Sherman became disgusted with the routine nature of army life and the slowness of promotion. Resigning his commission, he went into business, experienced failure, and in 1858 accepted the presidency of a military academy at Alexandria, Louisiana, a position in which he did well and resigned only when Louisiana left the Union in 1861. It was during this time that Sherman came to love the South and her people. But he felt that the Union must be preserved, though he had no feelings about slavery, and he wanted the war to end as quickly as possible with no punishment or retribution to follow the war.

Johnston had remained in the army and was given the prestigious command of the First Dragoons, the premier unit charged with patrolling and pacifying the frontier. After spending considerable time on the frontier trying to keep the peace between pro- and antislavery groups in Missouri and Kansas—a task Johnston handled with great fairness to both groups—he found himself promoted in June 1860 to the position of quartermaster general of the United States Army.

Ironically, at the beginning of the war, Sherman was in the South and was offered a commission in the Confederate army, while Johnston was in Washington, D.C., and was asked to keep his important post in the United States Army. Both men refused these offers and returned to their home states to find action on opposite sides.

Ironies would continue to dog the steps of these men. In the first major battle of the war, at Manassas, Virginia, both were present on the battlefield, Johnston commanding the Confederate forces and Sherman in charge of a brigade on the Union side.

Not long after Manassas, Sherman was sent to the western theater, where he would rise in rank and responsibility, although some people thought he was crazy because he frequently said the war would be a long and hard one. Assigned to duty in Kentucky, Sherman would face the challenge of controlling Confederate guerrillas before joining the main Union army in the West. Soon Sherman would become firm friends with his new commanding officer, Ulysses Grant. In April 1862, at the battle of Shiloh, Sherman would win a reputation for himself as a hard fighter.

In the East, where Johnston remained in command of Confederate forces in Virginia, the focus of the war shifted to the peninsula between the York and James Rivers. There Johnston faced the much larger army of George B. McClellan. As the Union army slowly advanced toward Richmond, Johnston saw an opportunity for a counterattack. On May 31, 1862, at the battle of Seven Pines, Johnston stopped the Federal advance but was seriously wounded. Following his recovery, Johnston was sent to the West as Confederate theater commander.

By 1864 the two men were commanding their side's largest armies in the western theater and would confront one another in one of the most hard-fought campaigns of the entire war. For over one hundred days, Sherman's command of about 120,000 men was in constant contact with Johnston's army of some 60,000 men. Every day brought combat and loss of life on both sides.

Because his force was larger, Sherman was able to pin Johnston's army in place and then try to outflank it; but every time Sherman tried, Johnston was able to wriggle out of Sherman's grasp and take up yet another defensive position. Whenever either army reached a new position, they would begin to make the dirt fly. Rail fences would be dismantled, the rails piled in a heap and dirt thrown over the pile. Logs would be added to the breastworks, while thousands of men loosened the dirt with bayonets, tin cups, or plates and heaped the earth on the fortifications with their bare hands. As soon as supply wagons came up, shovels and axes were passed out. The veterans of the campaign estimated that in eighteen hours they could have themselves eyebrow deep in trenches. Trying to capture such a position could be bloody work indeed. Soon both the men of Sherman's and Johnston's commands could tell by looking at an opposing line whether an attack had any chance of success. Neither army and neither commander could gain an advantage over the other in combat, they were so evenly matched.

Steadily, however, Sherman's maneuvers drew him closer to his ultimate objective, the city of Atlanta. Just before the two rival armies met in battle outside Atlanta, Johnston was relieved from command by the Confederate president, Jefferson Davis. Sherman would capture the city, but it was General John Bell Hood whose Southern army would suffer the defeat.

At the very end of the war, in the spring of 1865, Johnston was placed in command of the remnants of Confederate troops in the Carolinas. There he would oppose the triumphant Union forces under Sherman that had marched from Atlanta to the sea and had now turned north. It all came to an end on April 26, 1865, when Johnston yielded to Sherman's superior force in surrender.

Even then the two men showed how great had become the respect between them, for Sherman offered to Johnston the most generous of surrender terms. And after the war Sherman and Johnston became good friends.

On that cold, rainy February day when Johnston showed his respect for Sherman one last time by standing with uncovered head, Johnston did indeed catch his death. He took a cold that worsened into a respiratory infection. On March 21, 1891, Joseph Johnston joined William Sherman. Two opponents who had grown to respect each other were now united in death.

A LITTLE BIT OF DIXIE IN
WISCONSIN

1900

The four veterans of the Union army and two sons of Union veterans stepped slowly and carefully along the cemetery path as the bells of the Episcopal Church of Kilbourn, Wisconsin, tolled a farewell to the departed. On their shoulders they carried the coffin with the earthly remains of Belle Boyd, the most famous, romantic, and dashing female spy the Confederacy produced. The date was June 13, 1900.

Thirty-eight years earlier, on May 23, 1862, an excited eighteen-year-old girl ran across the fields and hills outside Front Royal, Virginia. Dodging patches of briars, stumbling over rocks, she dashed as fast as her long skirts would permit toward an advancing line of gray-clad infantry. Belle Boyd was convinced she had information that would allow the commander of those troops, General Thomas "Stonewall" Jackson, to make a successful attack on the village and its Union garrison. She would live in the light of the day's events the rest of her life. Delivering her message to a young staff officer she knew personally, Belle made her way back into the village as gunfire erupted around her.

Belle Boyd was born in Martinsburg, Virginia (West Virginia), on May 9, 1844. Her family was not wealthy, although her father, a merchant, had achieved a comfortable, middle-class status. Even as a child, Belle often shocked the household and her staid community by engaging in escapades unacceptable by the social mores of her day. She often went outside on the grass with bare feet and talked to male acquaintances as if she was their equal. When the war began in 1861, Belle and her family embraced wholeheartedly the Southern cause of independence. Her father, aged forty-four, closed his business and joined the Second Virginia Infantry as a private.

Perhaps Belle used her knowledge of the countryside and her network of friends on both sides of the Potomac River to make trips into Maryland and Ohio to bring back medicine and other items that were declared contraband of war by the Union authorities. If so, she was part of a stream of women and girls engaged in the same task. As to whether she actually carried any information to Stonewall Jackson at Front Royal remains an open question. Jackson had already made a surprise forced march on Front Royal, and his troops were moving forward in line of battle before Belle Boyd left the village to contact him. Her exploit might have gone unnoticed had she not been arrested.

Belle did something to catch the notice of the Federal authorities, and on July 30, 1862, she was arrested on orders from no less a person than Secretary of War Edwin M. Stanton. Taken to Washington under military guard, she was housed in the infamous Old Capitol Prison, a building noted for being overrun with lice and bedbugs. As was to be expected, Belle was hardly a model prisoner. Her cell was soon decorated with Confederate flags and pictures of various Southern leaders. When these decorations were confiscated by her jailers, Belle stood at her cell window overlooking a public street and sang "Dixie" and other Southern songs, always drawing an admiring audience.

Released after about a month, Belle went to Knoxville, Tennessee, and Montgomery and Mobile, Alabama, before returning to her home in the Shenandoah Valley. Following the Gettysburg campaign, as Union troops returned to Virginia, she was again arrested, this time spending four months in Union prisons before again going south.

In April 1864 Belle boarded the blockade runner *Greyhound* in Wilmington, North Carolina, in an attempt to reach England. Was this trip purely personal, or was she carrying secret dispatches to Confederate agents? We will never know because the *Greyhound* was captured, and all papers on board were destroyed to keep them from falling into Union hands. One Union officer boarding the *Greyhound* was Lieutenant Samuel Hardinge. Before the ship reached land, he and Belle were in love.

This alliance with the famous Belle Boyd alone might have caused trouble for Hardinge, but when the Confederate captain of the *Greyhound* escaped, suspicion of Hardinge's being unduly influenced by his fiancée became intense. Soon Hardinge was under arrest, while Belle found herself in exile in Canada.

More mysterious circumstances intervened, and somehow Hardinge and Belle found themselves in London, England, where, on August 25, 1864, the two became husband and wife. They had only a few months together before Hardinge, for some reason now unknown, returned to the United States. Soon he found himself again under arrest and a prisoner in Fort Delaware. On his release in early 1865, he returned to England and soon afterward died. Sam and Belle had a daughter, Grace, born only a few months before the death of her father.

Needing money on which to live, Belle prepared a manuscript that was published under the title *Belle Boyd in Camp and Prison.* The book was released just as the war was ending, and it became a success in Britain and in the United States. The book did much to establish the romantic aura with which Belle always surrounded her wartime exploits. Building on her fame as an author, Belle began a career on the stage, performing in theaters all over the United States.

In 1869 Belle found herself again in love, and again it was a Yankee who claimed her heart. Belle and John Hammond were married and remained together for fifteen years before what can only be called an amicable divorce ended their relationship in 1884.

In 1885 Belle married for the third time, to another Yankee, Nathaniel High of Toledo, Ohio. She also began working on a new phase of her career—a dramatic presentation of her wartime experiences. The show was first presented on February 22, 1886, and became an instant success in the North and South as now aging veterans relived, through her recitation, their own military careers.

On June 9, 1900, Belle arrived in Kilbourn, Wisconsin, as the guest of the local post of the Grand Army of the Republic. She was to give her dramatic program on June 11. Instead she suffered a heart attack and died.

Belle Boyd, famous Confederate spy, married in succession three Yankees and died in Wisconsin while the guest of an organization of Union veterans. Perhaps this is quite appropriate because Belle always ended her programs about her war experiences with the words, "One God—One flag—One people—Forever."

A concrete cap covers the grave of Belle Boyd. In the concrete is embedded a stone from each of the former Confederate states. The childhood home of Belle Boyd in Martinsburg, West Virginia, is now the headquarters of the county historical society and is open to the public.

THE WAR TAUGHT HIM
TO LOVE HORSES

1909

William Key was dying. He was seventy-six years old, and his closest companion was a horse, Beautiful Jim, which he called by his own last name, Key, because they were as close as brothers. William was proud of his horse because Jim was one smart horse; he could recognize the letters of the alphabet, spell words, add and subtract numbers up to twenty-five, distinguish between coins so as to make change, and play a small hand organ. William and Beautiful Jim Key had appeared at the Tennessee Centennial Exposition and had performed in New York City, New Jersey, and Atlantic City. But now the two old companions were to be separated by death.

"All I've got I owe to my love of horses. Even my life," William told his family. "If it weren't for being able to work with horses, the Yankees would have hung me in 1864." That was true, but ironic, because William Key had been born a slave and had remained, all his life, devoted to his former owners.

Even as a child on a farm in Franklin County, Tennessee, Key had shown unusual ability in working with animals, even training a pet rooster. He was so adept at breaking horses and teaching mules to pull plows that some people thought he had magical powers.

When the war came in 1861, Key, then twenty-eight years old, went with the two sons of his owner to "take care" of them. And take care he did. The regiment to which the two young men belonged was part of the garrison of Fort Donelson. When the fort was surrendered to Ulysses Grant's Union army in February 1862, Key found an unguarded path through the woods and helped the two white soldiers escape what would have been a trip to a prisoner of war camp. The two youths then joined the cavalry command of Bedford Forrest as scouts. Key found himself surrounded by horses. Soon the entire unit knew him as the best horse doctor connected with the Confederate army.

William Key's first brush with death came in the winter of 1862–63. Key and another black man were accompanying Forrest's command on a raid behind Union lines when they became separated from the Confederate forces. Trying to get back to Southern territory, the two men were apprehended by a Union army patrol from the Sixth Indiana and accused of being rebel spies. A drumhead court-martial condemned both men to death. Now Key and his friend had to think hard. How could they buy time?

During the Civil War small groups of soldiers, called "messes," did their own cooking. The army issued raw food and the men were expected to prepare it. Because most men had never handled a cooking pot, the food was usually pretty awful. Key's friend offered to cook for their guards and, overnight, found himself indispensable.

William Key then put his skills to work, healing sores on the horses' backs with a judicious use of homemade medicines and, in his spare time, playing poker with his guards. On the night before his execution, Key used his poker winnings, over one thousand dollars, to bribe a guard and escape.

When Key rejoined his young masters, he was regarded as one of the regiment and on the next raid was asked to go ahead of the unit by three days and scout their target. But again luck was against him. On the first day of his attempt to cross the Union lines, Key was arrested and recognized as an escaped condemned man, and the date of his execution was set for "dawn, the day after tomorrow." Key knew that sometime on the morning of his scheduled death day, the Confederates would attack the town where he was a prisoner. Again he had to delay his execution.

The officer commanding the men guarding Key was riding an obviously sick horse. Key talked one of the guards into letting him examine the horse and immediately saw that the problem was a minor one, which looked much worse than it really was. Key knew he could cure the animal in a matter of hours with ingredients readily available.

"Sir, I can cure your horse. I'm good with horses."

"How long will that take?"

"About forty-eight hours, only I ain't got that long before you all hang me."

"Well, go to work on the horse, and I'll see you get that long. But, don't try any tricks. You have escaped once and that won't happen again. Also, if the horse dies, you die at the same time."

"Sir, I understand. If the horse leaves, I leave."

Key began treating the horse, but at first he carefully used things he knew would do no good. He could not afford to be successful too soon. Then, as the time for the Confederate attack drew near, Key began the real treatment. Shortly after daylight on the day of his scheduled execution, Key had the officer's fully cured horse saddled and was riding him up and down before the officer's tent under the watchful eye of several guards, demonstrating the cure. Suddenly, the wild "rebel yell" cut through the morning air, and Confederate cavalry poured into the camp. Quickly, the Union officer found himself a prisoner.

"As I promised, sir," said Key, "when your horse leaves, I leave." And with those words Key rode away with the rest of the Southern force. William Key truly did owe his life to being able to work with horses.

After the war Key and the two young soldiers returned to Franklin County, Tennessee. The economy was in ruins and Key, now free in fact as well as in spirit, began to make a living training animals, practicing veterinary medicine, and playing poker. Within a few years he had earned enough money to purchase at a tax sale the farm where he had been a slave. He returned the farm to the sons of his former owner and paid for both of them to attend college. In 1890 a sickly colt was born to an Arabian mare Key had purchased for $40 from a bankrupt circus. That colt became the world-famous performing horse Beautiful Jim Key. With some of his income, Key started the Band of Mercy, a society dedicated to preventing cruelty to animals.

William Key is buried in the Willow Mount Cemetery in Shelbyville, Tennessee, a town today famous for its Tennessee Walking Horses. Beautiful Jim Key is buried not far from William under his own tombstone.

LITTLE SORREL'S STORY

1997

Throughout much of history, humans have formed bonds with animals, but perhaps no bond is as strong as that formed between people and horses. During the Civil War, when so much travel was done on horseback, and when rider and mount often died together, the bond between the two could become intense. Many stories have been told of this bond, Robert E. Lee with Traveler being the best known. But no story is more gripping than that of "Stonewall" Jackson and Little Sorrel.

Although Thomas Jonathan Jackson occasionally had been an amateur jockey as a boy, he was not considered a particularly good horseman in an age when equestrian skill was highly valued among soldiers. At West Point, Jackson was noted as having an awkward seat during cavalry drill, and he did not earn high grades in that area. Throughout his life, Jackson kept his stirrup leathers about six inches too short so that his knees were almost on a level with his mount's backbone.

Shortly after the Civil War began, Jackson was made a brigadier general and was sent to Harpers Ferry, Virginia, to organize and drill the raw recruits pouring into the area. One of his first acts was to stop rail traffic along the Baltimore and Ohio Railroad, seizing in the process several horses. Jackson's chief quartermaster, John Harman, picked out two horses and presented them to Jackson for his use. One was a rather large horse that became known as "Gaunt Sorrel," and the other, a smaller, medium-brown gelding, would become famous as "Little Sorrel." Actually, Jackson called the horse "Fancy," because the animal "suited his fancy." Although these horses were legitimate spoils of war, and Jackson was entitled to receive a horse for his military duties, he insisted on paying the Confederate government the full value of the mounts because they would be used for personal affairs as well as his duties.

A staff officer described Little Sorrel as "stocky, well made, round barreled, close coupled, good shoulders, excellent legs and feet, not fourteen hands high [less than fifty-six inches]. The horse was noted for being a natural pacer but was lacking in style. Sorrel had vast endurance and would eat whatever was offered him, whether hay or corncobs." It seems to have been this combination of temperament and easy gait that endeared Little Sorrel to Jackson. Later in the war Jackson was given a magnificent stallion, a true war-horse named "Superior," but this animal was relegated to the use of Jim, Jackson's African-American servant, while the general continued to plod along on Little Sorrel.

Jackson rode Little Sorrel at First Manassas, where the general received the title "Stonewall"; throughout the Valley campaign; he was astride the faithful animal at Cedar Mountain and Second Manassas; rode him along the lines at Fredericksburg; and was mounted on Little Sorrel on the evening of May 2, 1863, when he was mortally wounded by shots fired in the darkness by his own men.

Perhaps Jackson preferred to spend so much time riding Little Sorrel because the two shared so many characteristics. Jackson was notoriously indifferent to all food except fruit. When active, he would sometimes fail to eat at all for long stretches of time. As noted by one of Jackson's staff, Little Sorrel would eat anything from hay to corncobs. It soon became legendary in the Confederate army that Jackson could and would sleep anywhere, anytime. Jackson was notorious for going to church but sleeping through the sermon. Jackson could even sleep on horseback. Little Sorrel also took his rest seriously, lying down to rest whenever opportunity offered. Both horse and rider were unprepossessing in appearance, but when soldiers cheered or gave the rebel yell (the grandest music in the world, Jackson once said), both would pull themselves erect and be almost transformed in appearance. And in their baptism of fire at First Manassas, both the general and Little Sorrel suffered minor wounds.

Only twice did Jackson not have Little Sorrel with him when momentous events occurred. Once was during the Sharpsburg campaign when Jackson could not find his favorite mount, the horse having been stolen, only to be returned a few days after the bloody battle. Little Sorrel also missed Jackson's funeral, for when the general was shot out of the saddle, the horse ran away and was captured by a Union soldier, only to be recaptured a few weeks later.

Once back in Southern hands, Little Sorrel was sent to Mrs. Anna Morrison Jackson, who was at the home of her father, the Reverend J. G. Morrison, in Lincoln County, North Carolina. During and after the war, this family often used Little Sorrel both as a saddle horse and to pull a buggy.

Years rolled by and Mrs. Jackson found herself in difficult financial straits, so much so that the now aging Little Sorrel was a burden. In 1883 she sent Little Sorrel to the Virginia Military Institute (VMI), where her husband had been a professor before the war. The elderly horse, now in his thirties, seemed to enjoy having the run of the campus. When the Corps of Cadets turned out for rifle drill, he would trot up and down behind the lines, sniffing the gun smoke, and when the band played "Dixie," he would arch his neck and step as high as his arthritic legs allowed.

In 1885 a dispute over plans to send Little Sorrel to the World's Fair in New Orleans caused Mrs. Jackson to transfer ownership to the R. E. Lee Camp of United Confederate Veterans in Richmond. It was while in their custody that Little Sorrel died on March 16, 1886. Plans had already been made to have his hide mounted for permanent display, and this was quickly and expertly done.

By the late 1940s almost all the veterans were gone, and the R. E. Lee Camp was disbanded. Little Sorrel was again sent to VMI. Today, in the basement of Jackson Memorial Hall, Little Sorrel still stands—but without his bones.

When Little Sorrel died, his hide was preserved and mounted for display, and his bones were also preserved. Bones do not make an especially appealing museum display, so on July 20, 1997, 136 years to the day after Jackson rode Little Sorrel into immortality, becoming "Stonewall" Jackson on the field of Manassas, part of Little Sorrel was returned to the Virginia soil that had contained the remains of his master since 1863. In solemn ceremony, the members of the Corps of Cadets, Civil War reenactors, and visitors buried the bones of the faithful horse at the base of the life-size statue of Jackson on the VMI parade ground.

Hundreds of thousands of horses died during the Civil War. The honors paid Little Sorrel may well serve to honor them all. At last horse and master rest together in the soil of Lexington, Virginia.

Author's note: Special thanks is offered to the VMI Museum and its director, Colonel Keith Gibson, for assistance with this account.

A POTPOURRI OF
CIVIL WAR FACTS

- There was no declaration of war in the Civil War. Lincoln denied that the Confederacy was a legal entity, thus there was no one against whom to declare war. The southern states were, in Lincoln's view, being held hostage by rogue forces. Jefferson Davis did not seek a declaration of war because he thought the Confederacy was following the precedent set by the colonies in 1776, when they declared their independence without a declaration of war against Britain. The Union alleged the South started the war by firing on Fort Sumter, April 11, 1861. The Confederacy claimed the North started the conflict by committing an act of war in sending supplies to Fort Sumter.

- When the Civil War began, Minnesota was the first state to offer support troops to the Union.

- On the night before the battle of Stones River, the Union and Confederate armies sat only feet apart in the darkness while regimental bands played patriotic tunes. In a musical battle, the Confederates played "Dixie" and the Union soldiers played "The Battle Hymn of the Republic." Then both sides actually joined together for a rendition of "Home Sweet Home." When the song ended, both sides were silent, anticipating the battle to come.

- Through most of the war, General Robert E. Lee bivouacked in a tent stenciled 23RD NEW JERSEY INFANTRY, U.S. ARMY. It was a captured tent.

- General William T. Sherman did not utter his famous quote "War is hell" while in the midst of combat but in a speech he made in 1881.

- Confederate General Archibald Gracy was superintendent of streets in New York City when the war broke out.

- Confederate General Bushrod Johnson was a Quaker from Ohio.

- The first Confederate flag design had to be changed because it looked too much like the Stars and Stripes and confused soldiers in battle.

- Union major general George Thomas, the "Rock of Chickamauga," was a native of Virginia. His pro-Confederate sisters turned his portrait face to the wall, and it remained so until their deaths.

- Private George Culp was killed while fighting on his family farm during the battle of Gettysburg. Private Culp was in the Confederate army.

- Some Civil War–era cannon were capable of firing a shell weighing 125 pounds over a distance of five miles.

- During the war, for every man killed in combat, eight died of disease.

- At one time the North had over two million soldiers in its armies.

- Kansas, West Virginia, and Nevada were admitted to the Union during the war years.

- One Union general who served in Tennessee and Georgia was named Jefferson Davis.

- Abraham Lincoln's brother-in-law was a Confederate brigadier general. Benjamin Hardin Helm was killed in action at Chickamauga on September 20, 1863.

- When Alabama seceded from the Union, pro-Union Winston County attempted to secede from Alabama.

- The typical Civil War soldier was about five feet, seven inches in height, weighed 136 pounds, and had a thirty-six-inch chest when he breathed in.

- Before they became famous as the "Lightning Brigade" because of their use of repeating rifles, Colonel John Wilder's infantry brigade attempted to aid the Union cavalry by mounting mules used to pull the regiment's supply wagons—thus becoming "mounted infantry." The mules were unaccustomed to such treatment and quickly threw off the men attempting to ride them, much to the amusement of those gathered to watch.

- Civil War soldiers often carried a form of instant coffee in their haversacks.

- Another name for the battle of Lexington was the battle of the Hemp Bales.

- When he was drafted, President Grover Cleveland paid another man $150 to serve in his place.

- The only Confederate state capital to escape Union capture was Tallahassee.

BIBLIOGRAPHY

Alexander, Edward Porter. *Fighting for the Confederacy.* Edited by Gary W. Gallagher. Chapel Hill: University of North Carolina Press, 1989.

Bradford, Sarah H. *Scenes in the Life of Harriet Tubman.* 1869. Reprint. Salem, NH: Ayer Publishing Company, 1988.

Bradley, Michael. *Nathan Bedford Forrest's Escort and Staff.* Gretna, Louisiana: Pelican Publishing Company, 2006.

Catton, Bruce. *Glory Road.* New York: Doubleday & Company, 1952.

Cussler, Clive, and Craig Dirgo. *The Sea Hunters.* Part 6. New York: Simon & Schuster, 1996.

Dale, Edward Everett, and Gaston Litton. *Cherokee Cavaliers.* Norman: University of Oklahoma Press, 1939.

Davis, William C. *Duel Between the First Ironclads.* New York: Doubleday & Company, 1975.

Dawsey, Cyrus B., and James M. Dawsey, eds. *The Confederados: Old South Immigrants in Brazil.* Tuscaloosa: University of Alabama Press, 1995.

Douglas, Henry Kyd. *I Rode with Stonewall.* Chapel Hill: University of North Carolina Press, 1940.

Farwell, Byron. *Stonewall.* New York: W.W. Norton & Company, 1992.

Fox, Stephen. *Wolf of the Deep.* New York: Alfred A. Knopf, 2007.

Gara, Larry. *The Liberty Line: The Legend of the Underground Railroad.* Frankfort: University of Kentucky Press, 1961.

Hall, Richard. *Patriots in Disguise: Women Warriors of the Civil War.* New York: Marlowe and Company, 1994.

Krick, Robert K. *Stonewall Jackson at Cedar Mountain.* Chapel Hill: University of North Carolina Press, 1990.

Lement, Frank. *Dark Lanterns.* Baton Rogue: Louisiana State University Press, 1994.

Levy, George. *To Die in Chicago: Confederate Prisoners at Camp Douglas.* Evanston, Ill.: Evanston Publishing Company, 1994.

McKee, Irving. *"Ben-Hur Wallace": The Life of General Lew Wallace.* Berkeley: University of California Press, 1947.

McMillen, Lawrence. *The Schoolmaker: Sawney Webb and the Bell Buckle Story.* Chapel Hill: The University of North Carolina Press, 1971.

Oates, Stephen. *A Woman of Valor: Clara Barton and the Civil War.* New York: Free Press, 1994.

Ragan, Mark K. *Union and Confederate Submarine Warfare in the Civil War.* Mason City, Ia.: Savas Publishing Company, 1999.

Ramage, James A. *Rebel Raider: The Life of General John Hunt Morgan.* Lexington: University Press of Kentucky, 1986.

Robertson, James I. *Stonewall Jackson.* New York: Macmillan, 1997.

Root, George F. *The Story of a Musical Life.* Cincinnati: John Church Co., 1891.

Sigaud, Louis. *Belle Boyd, Confederate Spy.* Richmond, Va.: The Dietz Press, 1944.

Sinclair, Arthur. *Two Years on the Alabama.* New York: Konecky & Konecky, 2000.

Symonds, Craig L. *Joseph E. Johnston: A Civil War Biography.* New York: W.W. Norton & Company, 1992.

Taylor, John M. *Confederate Raider: Raphael Semmes of the Alabama.* Washington, D.C.: Brasseys, 1994.

Taylor, M. W. *Harriet Tubman.* New York: Chelsea House Publishers, 1991.

Vandiver, Frank. *Mighty Stonewall.* Austin: University of Texas Press, 1957.

Vandiver, Frank E. *Ploughshares into Swords: Josiah Gorgas and Confederate Ordnance.* Austin: University of Texas Press, 1952.

Wiggins, Sarah Woolfolk. *The Journals of Josiah Gorgas, 1857–1878.* Tuscaloosa: University of Alabama Press, 1995.

Work, George W. *Songs of Henry Clay Work.* New York: J.J. Little & Ives, 1884. Reprinted in 1920 and 1974.

Web sites

www.cwrc.org/c_war/singleton.html

www.west-point.org/taps/Taps.html

INDEX

ABOUT THE AUTHOR

Michael R. Bradley received a PhD in history from Vanderbilt University in 1970 and has taught at Motlow College in Lynchburg, Tennessee, since that time. He is the author of several collections of true Civil War stories, including *Old Times There Are Not Forgotten, To Live and Die in Dixie, Early on a Frosty Morn,* and *Land of Cotton.* Dr. Bradley has also written a history of an overlooked wartime campaign, *Tullahoma: The 1863 Campaign for Control of Middle Tennessee.* A member of the Tennessee Sesquicentennial Civil War Commission, he frequently leads tours of historic sites in Middle Tennessee.